God
is
Able

Fr. Pat Sheedy

First Edition

PAGE PUBLISHING
Conneaut Lake, PA

First originally published by Page Publishing 2023

The author does not need any profit from this book. Whatever profit may be realized from *God is Able* will 100 percent go to funding deepwater wells, building new schools in villages where there are no schools, and helping fund two medical/dental clinics in the area of Blessed Trinity Ocala's sister parish in Nalweyo, Uganda.

ISBN 979-8-88960-581-2 (pbk)
ISBN 979-8-88960-591-1 (digital)

Printed in the United States of America

This book is dedicated to all those who listen to God's voice,
who act on His word, and are astonished at how *God is Able* to work!

CONTENTS

Acknowledgments vii
Introduction ix
Section I: Noting the Nudges
Chapter 1: Early Roots of Letting God Be God 3
Chapter 2: The First Mission 9
Chapter 3: From the Farm to Florida 15
Chapter 4: Pack Your Bags 19
Section II: Watching God Work
Chapter 5: Uncharted Territory 23
Chapter 6: Along for the Ride 27
Chapter 7: No Strangers among Us 31
Chapter 8: I Confess 37
Chapter 9: Rest in Peace 41
Chapter 10: As He Passes By 45
Section III: Remaining on Course
Chapter 11: Stand There! 55
Chapter 12: Hail Mary 59
Chapter 13: Just Call Me Father 63
Chapter 14: When God Finds You 67
Chapter 15: When the Lights Go Out 75
Chapter 16: Carrying Crosses—Chosen and Unchosen 79
Section IV: The Need to Give
Chapter 17: Stewardship: God Is Number One 85
Chapter 18: Watch and Pray 89
Chapter 19: Putting God First 93
Chapter 20: Divine Direction 97
Chapter 21: Give-and-Take 101
Chapter 22: Filling the Gap 105

Chapter 23: Unexpected Help 109
Chapter 24: God's Loudest Voice 115
Section V: Go into the World
Chapter 25: God Is Able 119
Chapter 26: Uganda Revisited 123
Chapter 27: What Return Can I Make? 127
Chapter 28: Cape Town Blessings 131
Conclusion 135

ACKNOWLEDGMENTS

In July every year since 1965, I have gone to Ireland to visit family and friends and to get back to my roots and get renewed spiritually.

When COVID hit, I had to skip Ireland—no vacation in July 2020. With no thought of publishing a book, I spent some of my "free time" writing down my God experiences. The number of experiences grew and grew! I kept writing while traveling on planes and my days off over the following two years until my number of God experiences grew, and the idea of a book came into focus.

For me, it was not a burden to write. To get my notes in order and advance them to publication, I got 100 percent help from Ralph Ranieri, Mary Ann Rushing, Michelle Hernandez, Jim Ross, and Roz Smith. As a group, they reviewed and offered corrections and suggestions for each chapter. Once I found a publisher, Roz Smith took care of all the publishing details. The typing work was done by Melinda Gunn, who spent hours and hours typing and retyping each revised edition and making it available to us.

Without the help of each one of you, this book would not be published. Thanks, and God bless all of you.

INTRODUCTION

This book is not meant to be an autobiography. On my own, I have nothing much in my life that would grab anyone's attention for too long. On the other hand, when God is allowed to be God, there is a whole lot to write about that should grab the attention of anyone who is seriously striving to let God do His thing. The title of this book, *God Is Able*, is woven into each chapter.

For the most part, it is generally not that difficult, if we are tuned in, to see if some project or plan or decision under contemplation is of God or not—in other words, to see clearly if it actually promotes the kingdom if followed or if it damages or slows up the ongoing development of His kingdom.

I have always been influenced by Gamaliel, a Pharisee and celebrated doctor of Mosaic law, who gave sound advice to the Sanhedrin when they were trying to decide what to do with this man, Jesus of Nazareth. Basically, his advice was, if this man was not of God and did not speak for God, he would fail. But if he was of God, they were wasting their time, resources, and energy in trying to put him down, because they would not be able to stop him (Acts 5:38–39).

Just about all big ideas or projects in this book began with a clear insight or strong indication from God that He was giving us, whoever wanted to pay attention, work to do that would promote some aspect of His kingdom. Not only was the project approved by God, but He also guaranteed all the necessary ingredients to put the project on a successful course to final completion.

For the most part, one did not have to have all the resources, finances, and details figured out in advance to get to work. You will see that more clearly as you read several chapters of this book, such as the chapters on refugees, stewardship, missions, etc.

This is not in any way to say that there is no need for diocesan building boards, finance boards, liturgy boards, school boards, etc. All these are necessary for all diocesan projects that affect the lives of a multitude of people, that could put the diocese at risk, or that could fail to meet the desired goal. As Luke 14:28 says, "For which of you, when he wants to build a tower, does not first sit down and calculate the cost, to see if he has enough to complete it?"

The vast majority of our decisions in life, whether we are private individuals or in charge of a family or, like me, a pastor of a parish, does not require much more than sincere prayer and reflection and a humble willingness to say yes to God when He has more than adequately let us know what direction to take.

I believe we will all be shocked at the end when we finally find out God was clearly speaking directly to us, and we were not tuned in. We were otherwise too engaged in nonessentials, or we were tuned in, but we were not ready to disturb our comfort zone to follow God's direction.

Very often, when God makes His wishes or makes His plans known to us, it will mean we have to step out of our comfort zone. If we do, the results are beyond our wildest dreams. The trouble is stepping out of our comfort zone.

Early on in my life, I stepped way out of my comfort zone—not because I had the courage to do so or because I saw it as God's holy will but, quite the opposite, because I didn't have the courage to say no, which I dearly wanted to say. I didn't ever want to be in the limelight.

Years and years later, I now see those times when I stepped out against my will as God setting the stage for His future plans for me. My sincere advice now to those who lack self-esteem or courage is to step out of their comfort zone when they clearly see that this decision will advance their life for the better. God will always provide what you need when you step out.

So the purpose of this book is to help you tune in to God and let God be God. Go with Him when He makes His way clear, and never worry about the results.

Section I

Noting the Nudges

My grace is sufficient for you, for power is made perfect in weakness.

—2 Corinthians 12:9

CHAPTER 1

EARLY ROOTS OF LETTING GOD BE GOD

I had the big advantage of being raised with eleven brothers and sisters on a 160-acre multipurpose farm in County Clare, Ireland, with a Catholic mom and dad. Work was never a big deal. It was what we all did. It was so easy to see that your work, with and for the family, was truly meaningful for the good of the family.

Our dad, who came within two years or so of being an ordained priest, inspired us to fully use our educational opportunities. We all went as boarders to a convent or diocesan secondary schools. The family didn't have the money for all that tuition, but our dad made bargains with the schools by supplying turf (pent) in lieu of money.

We had about forty acres of bogland on our farm. We all took part in cutting and saving the turf, turning it for drying and then stacking it, and filling it into lorries for the schools. In a way, we were taking a big part in paying for our own high school tuition. That was no big deal. It was what everyone did. Years later, I saw it as a big preparation by God for me, for us, to be a team player in the work of the church.

One little story that happened to me personally that influenced letting God be God in my life was when our class took the state test for all sixth-graders. The results gave the secondary school the information needed to place students at the level they could handle academically. It so happened that I got the highest grade of the six to eight students in our village school.

The local priest, Father Sexton, came in and talked to the headmaster privately, but I sensed they were talking about me. They called me up and announced I had received the highest grade in the class. I couldn't believe it. I was extremely shy, lacking in confidence, and very much an introvert. I still am an introvert, but most people do not believe that about me.

Father Sexton had, in my eyes, a huge can of hard candy, which he gave to me to take home to our family. I got a bit of a boost in confidence and brought the big tin of hard candy home. I've forgotten what Dad said to begin with, but almost immediately, he suggested that I take the tin of hard candy back to the school to share it with all the other students.

That continues to say a lot to me about the blessings of life. They are not all for personal use or glory or fame but to be shared to others. A tin of hard candy would not be a big deal today. But for the students of the school in the village where we all grew up, the hard candy was an unusually big treat.

During my five years—that was the Irish system—in secondary boarding school, I continued to be a shy, backward, very much introverted student. Most of my brothers and sisters were athletes and involved in one sport or another. I was always interested in all sports, and I still am. But in secondary school, you had to play unless you had a doctor's cert that excluded you. This was a problem for me.

So I decided to stand at the goal as the goalie thinking wrongly it would be the easy way for me to comply with the school rules. Much to my total surprise, I turned out to be a halfway decent goalie and served as class goalie for my class in Irish hurling, Irish football, and soccer for all five years of high school and all six years in the seminary.

On the days when you were excused from contact sports but still had to play some sport, another farmer's son, Martin, and I would practice handball. We were not skillful, but we were tough and whacked the ball with all our developed farmer's muscles. We joined the school handball league.

Our opponents, who were not aware of any notable skills we had, would play us expecting to walk over us and move on to the next round. To their shock, we kept winning and winning and then were finally knocked out in the semifinal. That sport was a real blessing to me up to the age of sixty-five. I had to move from handball to racquetball (reluctantly) because racquetball in the US quickly took over handball.

Looking back, I thank God that, unknown to me at the time, He provided me with a sport that I took on very reluctantly but has been a big blessing to my health for more than fifty years. Learning from that, today, I continue to urge all students to get involved in competing in some sport. It was easy for us in our teen years. We had no choice. Unfortunately, students today have a choice to play or not to play. I always encourage young people to listen to their parents. Get rid of a lot of the time spent on gadgets and play some sport. They don't have to be good enough to represent the school team. It will not only be good for their physical health, but it will also be a real blessing to their overall self-esteem.

During my fourth year in secondary school, I was selected for a student leadership job. It wasn't much of a job, but at the time, it was a big deal to me. I was appointed by the dean of students to oversee and take charge of the boot hall—the equipment hall. I was even given the keys! Me, given the keys! Me who sat in each class quietly, out of sight, and never asked questions and never wanted to speak in public. God was again at work.

In my fifth and final year in secondary school, I was selected as one of the seven prefects. Our job was to represent the student body's concerns and bring them to the school authorities. We also had to ask the dean for movies or a half day or a full day off for the students. You couldn't do that today. One such event still stands out in my mind.

The students convinced me that we were all due a day off. They pushed me to go on my own and present their petitions. Not wanting to let them down, even though I was lacking in confidence to proceed, I shyly pushed ahead with my knees knocking against each other. I presented the student request to the dean. To my surprise, he granted the request. That was another conviction for me to step out of my comfort zone and see good results follow.

Sight unseen before entering the seminary, we were all given a number from one to forty-three, the number of freshmen in our class. To my surprise and still unknown to me, I was given number one. So for six years, I represented the class in all matters that pertained to our class. In the final year, another seminarian, Martin, and I were selected by the dean to represent the more than two hundred seminarians before the college staff.

God is always sowing seed. I can't take much credit for accepting His lead. I did it because the opposite was unthinkable. Reflecting on God's opportunities presented to me, I gradually saw I could trust Him, and He would work out the details.

My son, hold fast to your duty, busy yourself with it, grow old while doing your task.

—Sirach 11:20

CHAPTER 2

THE FIRST MISSION

My conscience told me—or God told me—I should branch out from my very confined local Irish countryside upbringing if I was going to have any chance at all to make some kind of a meaningful, priestly existence in faraway Florida.

So another seminarian, Paddy, and I hitchhiked most of our way to London to work for the summer weeks when we were in first theology class. We had no plan, but we both found a construction job—me with pick and shovel down in the trenches and him as the canteen man. We worked ten hours a day. It was the only job/work in all my life that I did not find meaningful.

We learned that the Irish in London were the best workers. They were reliable, they used crude, rough language, and many of them spent a good bit of time in the pub. They were not as faithful to Sunday mass as the Irish in Ireland at that time were, but I learned from it, and because of it, I grew a deep appreciation for the countless people who went to work every day just because and only because they needed the pay to survive as families.

Paddy and I went further. We decided to take a pub job for four hours each night. We wanted to experience how the Irish in London lived their lives. Neither of us had ever tasted alcohol. We had a permanent pledge to abstain for life. (I still have mine.)

Since many of the Irish, men especially, tended to abuse alcohol, a spiritual movement was started in Dublin by the Jesuits. These

Jesuits reached out to all youth at about age fourteen, asking them to abstain from all alcohol for two years. At age sixteen or older, you could make that a permanent pledge.

It was called the Pioneer Total Abstinence Association. All members wore a Sacred Heart pin and said a daily prayer of commitment. While I do not wear the Sacred Heart pin anymore, because I get too many questions, I still keep the pledge.

We made some good money, in our estimation, from both jobs. When we got home, I gave it all to my parents because, after all, that was the way we were raised, and someone in the family had to do the farmwork I would have done had I stayed home instead of going off to London for a good time!

My bishop in Florida forbade us to go work in London the second summer, so a number of us joined a Legion of Mary group (*Peregrination Pre Christi*, or wandering for Christ) and went to a parish in Aylesbury, England, to work under a parish priest, Canon John Galvin, from Cork, Ireland.

Canon Galvin sent me and Tom, a seminarian from Cork, out on our bicycles to a village, Aston Abbots, seven miles from Aylesbury. Our assignment was to visit every family in the village and take up a census and let Canon Galvin know the name, address, phone, etc. of every Catholic family in the village. We had never knowingly met anyone but Catholics where we grew up. We grew up with 100 percent Catholics.

We went down one side of the village, walking in the footpath to the door of each residence, walking back out the same footpath to the sidewalk, and walking down the sidewalk to the footpath to the next residence. After hours of this walking in, out, down, and in again, we decided to shorten our walks by just crossing the lawn to the next door.

Mrs. Taylor was inside the window, looking out at us walking on her immaculate lawn. We had none of them in Ireland.

Before we even reached her door, she, with fire in her eyes, had opened it and said, "How dare you walk on my lawn!"

With heads bowed, we said nothing.

Then she said, "What are you here for anyway?"

We explained we were taking up a census and making a record for Canon Galvin of all the Catholics in the area. Her temper cooled down, and she said she was C of E (Church of England). We ended up having a nice conversation with Mrs. Taylor.

At the end of the village was a convent of nuns, C of E nuns. We had only heard of Catholic nuns. The holy water font was inside the door, and the tabernacle lamp was lit. The nuns genuflected, and so did we. I still remember our conversation with the three C of E nuns. They were hoping, expecting, and praying that the C of E and the Catholic church would fully reunite in their lifetime! It still has not happened. If anything, we are more divided now from each other than we were back then in 1963.

Next summer, we were back again in Aylesbury, doing our Legion of Mary work. Canon Galvin sent me and Tom out on our bicycles to Aston Abbots, this time just to revisit the Catholic families we had identified the previous year. We brought our notes with us from last year.

As we passed Mrs. Taylor's house, we said, "Let's revisit Mrs. Taylor."

This time, we did not walk on her lawn.

Her seventeen-year-old daughter answered the doorbell and said, "Mum is in the hospital back in Aylesbury."

That evening, Tom and I rode our bikes to the hospital in Aylesbury and visited Mrs. Taylor. She gave us a huge welcome. I kept in touch with Mrs. Taylor. She and her second daughter, Susan, age sixteen, came as guests to Ireland to the double wedding ceremony of my sister and brother in 1967, two years after my ordination. Susan and her husband, Malcolm, came to the fiftieth anniversary (golden jubilee) of my brother's and my ordination in Ireland in 2015. Susan and her family are still very active C of E.

My third summer back in Aylesbury, I was now a newly ordained priest. Canon Galvin invited three of us—Jim, Martin, and me (Tom had quit the seminary)—to give a two-week mission. Looking back, I still find it difficult to believe why we, newly ordained greenhorns, were asked and then said yes! Each day of the mission, one of us celebrated the mass, one preached the homily, and one was available for sick calls.

One evening, when I was on sick call duty, I got a call to the local hospital. I went on my bike. Mrs. Phil O'Sullivan had just delivered her baby, Geraldine. Both mother and baby were in a critical stage. I anointed Mrs. O'Sullivan (my first anointing) and baptized Geraldine (my first baptism).

Here we are fifty-six years later, and we are still in touch. I did Geri's wedding in Aylesbury to Rolf when she was twenty-five. I gave First Communion to her first son, Ben, in Aylesbury when he was seven years old.

I visit Aylesbury every second year on my way to Ireland. That visit always includes four stops—one to Geri and Rolf and their entire family, one to Mrs. Taylor's daughter Susan and Malcolm and their family, one to the family Canon Galvin put me to stay with each mission to Aylesbury: the O'Grady/Downs family, and finally, Henry O'Callaghan, who made me comfortable with all kinds of pastoral work in a parish.

Legion of Mary missions to Aylesbury gave me much-needed confidence, many insights into pastoral work, including prison work, and a great love for all the possible faithful work a priest could be immersed in.

At the time, since I had already been accepted as a priest for the Diocese of St. Augustine, Florida, I thought I had made a mistake. I loved working in England even though it was only for a few weeks each summer.

But I hadn't been too long in the US when I clearly saw that it didn't matter where you were. If you put your mind to it, you could serve God anywhere.

For I know well the plans I have in mind for you, says the Lord, plans for your welfare, not for woe—plans to give you a future full of hope.

—Jeremiah 29:11

CHAPTER 3

FROM THE FARM TO FLORIDA

I loved farming. Until I was about seventeen, there was no other career in my mind but farming. But I would not have turned out to be a successful farmer. I would have had little or no trouble doing all the labor. My dad was ahead of all of us. He had spent years in the seminary and was within two years of being ordained. But he never told us that; we found out years later.

My dad just knew that my next brother, Dan, had all the gifts and creativity to be a good, successful farmer. He could move on with all the new farming techniques that were just coming in for those who wanted to move ahead or be left behind. I would have been left behind.

We had three uncles who were priests and three aunts who were nuns. At about age seventeen and a half, it suddenly came to me that God was calling me into the priesthood. I never doubted that once God made the call clear. I only worried about where I would serve. I didn't like languages, except Gaelic, so I excluded all countries that didn't speak English. Ireland had too many priests then (not now). We were brought up with a bit of a prejudice against England, to put it mildly. At the time, Australia and New Zealand were far, far away.

With no clear plan in my head, a priest came from Miami looking for recruits. Florida at the time (1958) had just been divided into two dioceses. This Miami priest was immaculately dressed and had no time for private questions after his talk. A few of us who were interested put him out of our minds.

The next priest who came recruiting was also from Florida, a pastor of a church in Lake City. He was Irish born and was very down-to-earth. He told us nothing about sunshine, beaches, tourism, etc. He told us he traveled over two hundred miles each Sunday to say four masses in four different churches. His area had less than 5 percent Catholics.

Where we grew up, it was 100 percent Catholic. We saw the big need. Four of us signed up on the spot. We didn't need to know anymore. Three of the four of us were ordained for the Diocese of St. Augustine six years later.

My family had half expected me to go on for priesthood. My brother Micko (Michael), who was big on playing sports and playing jokes and who was very much an extrovert, caused a surprise to our family when he declared he was going into the priesthood. He was going to Maynooth, the National Seminary, and going to work in our home diocese of Killaloe.

Micko was seven years in the seminary. I was six years at St. Patrick's, Carlow, Ireland. At the time, all ordinations took place with your entire class. My ordination was set for one week before his ordination. We got permission from his bishop to have Micko's ordination with my class in Carlow.

But the bishop added, "You can also be ordained together by me at your local parish, St. Senan's Church, Cooraclare, County Clare, at a regular Sunday mass."

That was unheard of at the time, another one of those God things that you never expected or dreamed of.

The day was so special for our parents, our entire family, all the people we grew up and went to school with, and the entire parish community. And to crown it all off, the day was June 13, the same day our mom and dad got married thirty years ago. How could we have been so blessed? Even to this day, we still do not have ordinations in the local parish of the person being ordained.

Now more than fifty-six years later, when I go home and do my annual tour among extended family, some of them still remember even the minutest details of our ordination day. I'm sure God was saying much more to me on June 13, 1965, my ordination day, than I grasped at the time. The magnitude of God's blessings all too often takes years to sink in.

As for me to be near God is my good, to make the Lord God my refuge.

—Psalm 73:28

CHAPTER 4

PACK YOUR BAGS

Archbishop Hurley was the bishop of St. Augustine. We all knew he assigned the new priest—you had no input—to Catholic University for further studies after one year in a parish. By now, I was loving being a priest at Resurrection. I was just convinced that God wanted me to stay on at Resurrection, and I just knew Archbishop Hurley could easily see the same.

But no, I was told, "Pack your bag and be a student at CUA in Washington, DC."

Three other priests in the area also got a CUA assignment. We bought a 1953 Buick for $160, $40 each. I was given the task of driving the 1953 Buick to DC. Feeling sorry for myself, I set out for DC and prayed, and it came to me.

"You can be miserable, or you can adjust and be happy!"

By the time I had driven halfway to DC, I had already realized I could be happy anywhere if I went with God. I loved my year at CUA.

My thesis for my master's in religious education was *The Role of the Priest in Racial Integration*. I had the privilege of interviewing several interracial couples. That has helped over the years in promoting the Catholic church's teaching that all people are created special and equal by God. No one race or group or religion is superior or above others. We can all, without knowing it, have built-in prejudices that hinder our work in God's kingdom.

Living in Washington, DC, for a year greatly helped me to love and appreciate the US. It also made me realize that since we were so blessed in so many ways as a country, we had the responsibility and the privilege of reaching out and uplifting other people or countries that were really struggling to provide the very basics for their people.

The great Bible story of the Good Samaritan came more alive for me—that we were our brother's keeper. I was able to expand President John F. Kennedy's (RIP) famous quote: "Ask not what your country can do for you but what you can do for your country and the world."

Section II

Watching God Work

The problem with the world is that we draw the circle of our family too small.

—St. Teresa of Calcutta

CHAPTER 5

UNCHARTED TERRITORY

I was assigned to Our Lady of Lourdes, Daytona, and to the teaching staff at Father Lopez Catholic High School in 1967.

At Father Lopez, in my senior-level religion classes, I had three black students who were not Catholic. They quickly saw I was not prejudiced and had several outside-of-class conversations with me on the topic of racial prejudice. They were good athletes but were also very strong academically.

They used to talk freely about who was and who was not prejudiced among the faculty. I was not aware and not that perceptive, but they could easily read negative body language. They were not critical or complaining, just observing.

In the course of our conversations, they asked me if I would accept an invitation to Bethune–Cookman College to meet the whole student body and staff. One of the students' dad had a big job at Bethune–Cookman. I told them I didn't feel I had much to offer. They insisted and asked me if for their convocation at the college I would say a Catholic mass. That I could do.

We prepared handouts for the students so they could follow. We gave a list of hymns to their choir. We had a fully participated mass by their students and faculty. I made one announcement. If anyone was interested in getting to know more about the Catholic faith, I would lead an inquiry class on campus at 8:30 p.m. every Wednesday.

Approximately fifteen students showed up every Wednesday, but not at eight thirty!

They started coming in around 9:00 p.m., and classes began at about 9:10 p.m. After a few weeks of my waiting on my own for half an hour, I asked if it would be okay if we moved the time to 9:00 p.m. I would be fine with that time, and since many of them were coming in from sport activities, etc., it might have suited everyone better. They replied as a group. No, they wanted to keep the time at eight thirty! I did. I was still the only one present until 9:00 p.m., so I showed up at 9:00 p.m. from then on.

We concluded the class, and about twelve of the students were received into the Catholic faith. I was only at Father Lopez's school and parish for one year, so I lost track of whether they did or did not continue in the Catholic faith, but the whole encounter with Bethune–Cookman College was a big *God thing* for me.

At that time, spring break for hundreds of thousands of college students happened at Daytona Beach. There was no room to allow thousands of churchgoing Catholics into the local Catholic churches. They spilled out into the parking lots. This was the chatter I kept hearing from the local priests.

A friend suggested to me, "Why don't we celebrate an open-air mass on the beach on Easter Sunday morning?"

It so happened a very professional Catholic song leader and guitarist presented herself to lead the music.

The open-air band shell, which seated five thousand, was crowded for mass. Some local priests were hesitant about the whole idea. Students wouldn't be dressed properly, etc. While I was officiating, I saw three priests sitting on the low wall around the band shell, observing. All the five thousand who showed up were dressed in their Easter best, except for three students, who were in swimsuits.

Now fifty-three years later, that mass is still being celebrated. Sometimes, we just go with God without knowing all the details in advance.

You shall treat the alien who resides with you no differently than the natives born among you; have the same love for him as for yourself; for you too were once aliens in the land of Egypt. I, the Lord, am your God.

—Leviticus 19:34

CHAPTER 6

ALONG FOR THE RIDE

After one year in Daytona, when I came back from my usual vacation in Ireland, I was greeted by my pastor.

"Welcome back. By the way, you are moving next weekend!"

I called the bishop, and he said, "Yes, I'm moving you to Lakeland. You have been three years there in Daytona."

"But, Bishop, I'm only here one year!"

"Well, I'm moving you anyway to St. Joseph's!"

Yes, God had spoken through the bishop.

In 1975, when Vietnam fell and thousands of Vietnamese refugees were pouring into the US, the daily papers were calling out for help for the more than thirty thousand at Eglin Air Force Base. A visiting Irish priest, Father Mike Conway, from the Diocese of Motherwell in Scotland, had a chat with me at breakfast one day.

He said, "Let's go up to Eglin AFB to see what this is all about."

Was this God letting us know to get moving? There was no need to delay any longer. The refugees needed our response.

We phoned another couple, Tony and Ruby, and another young lady, Judy, and drove to Eglin AFB. We had the name of one young Vietnamese girl who spoke English and who had applied for a job at Florida Southern College in Lakeland. We had no real plan, just taking a look.

As we walked through thousands of refugees, making our way to the control camp, we were being begged to sponsor many of them.

But we put them all off since we had decided to look for the family of the Vietnamese girl who spoke English. The control camp found the family within minutes.

There were twenty-two in the family: Grandpa and Grandma, their two sons and their wives, fourteen grandchildren, and two cousins. I signed the papers as their sponsor, and as yet, we had no plans in place. We even brought the two oldest granddaughters, Nga and Mai Phuong, the one who spoke English, home with us to Lakeland. They stayed with Tony and Ruby until we got the rest of the family to Lakeland.

We never had a parish meeting. Settling the refugees was not on the parish council agenda. But things began to fall into place with miraculous speed. We rented a large six-bedroom house from the owner for $125 a month. He had asked for $275, but it was in very poor condition. We said we would get rid of all the junk and paint and repair the house and furnish it as long as he dropped the rent to $125 for as long as the family lived there. He was a good Catholic, he agreed.

Over thirty-five volunteers showed up the next Saturday, doing the repairs and painting. English tutors were lined up. A good Catholic car mechanic volunteered to search for good secondhand cars. Others got involved in seeking employment.

The government gave the sponsoring church money to settle each refugee. We got good at it. It cost the parish nothing, except thousands of volunteer hours. The refugees were great workers. They learned English fast. We bought cars, eighteen in all. Each Vietnamese owner paid us back at the rate of ten dollars a week. They all paid back in full. One owner of a fish factory in Winter Haven took a chance and hired two ladies who did not speak English. They worked out so well that we could not supply the owner with enough refugee workers.

In all, we sponsored 140 refugees, and we convinced a Catholic pastor in Winter Haven to also sponsor a large family. The young Vietnamese all went to college and did very well. One husband of a family we sponsored became a deacon in the Diocese of Orlando and still works for the church.

Again, when some project, such as sponsoring refugees, is obviously from God, why not go with it? Do we have to line up everything in advance before we say yes? If it is obviously a *God thing*, leap out in faith. Don't worry, it will work out. How could it not succeed? All that is required is an enthusiastic yes. God glorifies the effort put into the project.

I was in prison and
you visited me.
—Matthew 25:36

CHAPTER 7

NO STRANGERS AMONG US

During our visits to Aylesbury, we developed a very nice friendship with Father Paddy Glenn, who was the local prison chaplain. He was chaplain to four prisons, one of which was a very high-security prison.

I'll never forget my first visit to the high-security prison. Father Paddy and I and the jailer were walking along, going through one clanging prison gate after another. The jailer opened a strong, noisy door to a prison cell with one inmate. The cell was about six feet by nine feet.

Father Paddy said to me, "Okay, you go in and talk to him. We'll be back later."

And they locked me in with the inmate!

I learned a lot from that one experience. I have been visiting state and federal prisons and jails now for almost sixty years. It is easy work. It is very fulfilling. For the most part, most all the inmates I have been in touch with have real, genuine needs and will advance to a normal, productive life if given half a chance. I have had a few notable experiences.

I used to say mass at Polk Correctional. A hit man for the mafia who was on Florida's death row for a time but got out when Florida suspended death row for a brief few years was my altar boy. He used to be a staunch anti-Catholic and studied the Catholic faith to have more ammunition to fight the church. In the process, he became

Catholic. By the time I met him, he was well-known and praised by two bishops and hoped to become a Catholic deacon when he got out. He got out, but I had no idea what happened to him then.

When I said mass in an Orange County jail, I was stopped by a head prison guard at the gate, because I had a very small bottle of wine for the consecration.

He said, "Alcohol is not allowed."

But I said, "I have to have it for Catholic mass. We always have a little wine."

He said, "I'm in charge. Leave now."

So I left.

I reported the incident to the Irish nun who at the time was in charge of Catholic services for prisons and jails. She was tough.

She said, "Leave it to me. I'll take care of it."

Next month, I was back for mass. I met the same tough security guard.

"I told you, you cannot bring in alcohol," he said.

But I insisted, "Sir, if you look in your notes, you will see Catholic priests are allowed to bring in wine for mass."

"No. Leave now," he said.

So I went out to my car and poured a little wine in a thimble, left the little bottle of wine in my car, put the thimble full of wine in my pocket, and came back to the security gate.

Now I said, "May I enter?"

He said, "Yes, go ahead."

So I went and said mass with my thimble full of wine. The Irish nun straightened him out later.

I was saying mass in a jail once, and one man sat way in the back on his own. He was a federal prisoner. I went back and asked him if he would like to join us up near the front. He said not really. There was nothing much going on, on the fed's side of the jail, so he thought it might be nice for a change. His name was Mick. Well, Mick came again and again and finally moved up front. He was Catholic.

He was moved to several prisons in other states and wrote to me from each one. He even had his wife write to me from the Midwest. The feds couldn't break him down. He finally completed his nineteen years or so and got out. He invited me to a dinner with his wife about one hundred miles away from where I was assigned.

During dinner, a man from a nearby table, where there were six men at dinner, came over to me and said, "Aren't you Father Pat? All six of us over here are priests."

I went to join them for a ten-minute chat.

After dinner, Mick shook hands with me and secretly passed five hundred dollars on to me.

A few days later, I had a phone call from one of the six priests, who asked, "Who was that couple you had dinner with?"

"Why?" I said.

"Well, the man went to the cashier while you were talking to us and paid for all six of us and another round of drinks and dessert!"

The following year, I met Mick and his wife and their daughter in another city.

Mick said, "Susie is getting married in a year and a half. Will you come to our state and officiate at the wedding?"

I said, "I'd love to, but that week, we celebrate my mom's ninetieth birthday, so I know I will be in Ireland."

He phoned me back a week later and said they had changed the date.

"Now will you come?"

Why not?

Mick and his wife became great supporters of the church and our mission in Uganda.

While hearing confessions at Lowell Correctional, one young lady—her crime was public—told me she had killed her mother. I didn't act shocked. Then she came to Communion.

Then after mass, she came up to me and said, "Can I be Catholic?"

I said, "You have just been to confession and Communion. Are you baptized?"

No, she said, so I told her she had to wait and take some instructions first and get baptized. We promised her help. She was moved to a Tallahassee prison, and there she convinced the priest to baptize her at the Easter Vigil, and he put me down as her godfather.

Heather had two children at nineteen before she went to prison. She spent about eighteen years in prison. She stayed in touch with me as she moved from prison to prison. I met her when she got out and took her shopping.

She has been married twice since then and has not been in trouble. She has two more kids, whom I baptized at Blessed Trinity. For her, after all those years in prison and an extremely difficult upbringing, life is still very tough. She came to my golden jubilee mass and was introduced to the community and got a big welcome.

While I was attending a Vatican II course near San Francisco, the chaplain at San Quentin wanted a weekend off and asked if one of us would volunteer to say the mass. I offered and asked him to get permission for me to go to death row, which was also within the prison. I said mass with the regular inmates.

The Irish Christian brother with us had permission to go to death row, but he forgot to get me cleared.

I said, "Well, I'll walk along with you."

"But," he said, "you will not get in."

I said, "Don't worry. I'll walk along and see what happens."

Security checked him out and patted him up and down, front and back, and said, "Okay, you can go in."

I walked along with him, and they never even asked me my name, another *God thing* I could never explain.

The Christian brother said, "We have permission to talk to this one Catholic on death row."

I said, "You talk to him. I'll walk down the corridor and talk to whoever wants to talk. No one is paying any attention anyway."

I still remember all four death row inmates I met through a seven-by-fourteen-inch opening in each door. Two of them had no interest at all in the outside world and did not watch the news on their little TV sets, only old movies and comedy. The other two were praying for the possibility of one day having a productive life. They were reading books, keeping themselves physically fit, watching the news on TV, and hoping for a second chance.

It is such a blot on our states that still allow capital punishment. There is no good reason for it now. Years ago, it was judged necessary to ensure the safety of everyone when the inmate was judged to be a permanent danger. But now we can permanently put a dangerous inmate away for life in a way that he/she can be no danger to anyone.

It costs many times more money to enforce the death penalty than to keep the person in prison for life. It actually costs five times more money to bring a person to his death by whatever means they are using, mostly because of the years—years of court cases, appeals, etc. And worse still, the death penalty brings out the worst in us—an "eye for an eye" type of mentality.

God never gives up on anyone. While we have a duty to keep our society safe, we can still do that, save money, and give the dangerous death row inmate an opportunity to come back to God.

I was a stranger and
you welcomed me.

—Matthew 25:35

CHAPTER 8

I CONFESS

Hearing confessions about fifty years ago, I couldn't help but detect that a few regular penitents came and confessed behind the screen but had an accent that was not foreign or typically American. I had heard a similar accent in Ireland, but it wasn't an Irish accent. It was the accent of an Irish Traveller, known in Ireland as tinkers.

I had an opportunity to meet a few of them outside the confessional room. That began what has become a special fifty-year spiritual friendship between them—there are about seven thousand of them in the US—and me.

The Irish Travellers, for the most part, had to leave Ireland in the 1840s because of the famine that left millions starving to death. They were already thrown off the land in Ireland, so when they came to the US, they traveled in travel trailers to wherever they found work.

They are all self-employed; they seal and stripe parking lots, paint, and do some minor roofing jobs, paving, etc. Most of their work is given to them by repeat customers, because for the most part, they get good references. A few may cheat, and those few give them an undeserved bad name to the police in many states. The media tend to pick up on that.

They are all strong, active Catholics. They believe very much in daily family prayer. They go to confession often—every few weeks. They go to Catholic mass wherever they happen to be every Sunday.

They do not live together before marriage. They are all virgins getting married. They grow up fast and are really ready for marriage at a much younger age than most all other cultures. Most of their schooling is done at home after they complete the fifth grade. Normally, they plan to marry within their culture, so they do not date outside their culture.

I officiate at many of their weddings, baptisms, and some funerals. Some weddings can be very small with only a bride and groom, and I find two witnesses. Some are large with three or four hundred people and more than thirty bridesmaids and groomsmen. I have been to at least fifteen states to officiate at their weddings. I try to help them, and they very much help me and the broad mission of the church, including our Uganda mission. Three of them have actually come on one mission trip to Uganda with us.

Like all of us, they have their faults. Some men may drink too much; some like to compete with the Joneses. A few may take advantage of work clients. Some women may put pressure on their men for nice clothes, jewelry, etc. They gossip, but who doesn't?

We have a lot to learn from them. They 100 percent believe in marriage and will rarely, if ever, get a divorce, if at all possible. They are aware of their faults (sins), and so frequent confession challenges them. Intimate sexual relationship is totally reserved for a husband and wife who have celebrated their marriage in church at a Catholic mass. It is what God asks of us. Could we—will we—ever get back to God's way?

The Travellers have numerous stories of areas in the US where police are regularly trying to trap them into crime or stopping them on the road, looking for something to convict them for. In the year 2000, I had a request from one Traveller family for confirmation for their thirteen-year-old daughter.

"And what about her first cousin? Could she be added? And what about..."

Eventually, the what-abouts reached one hundred for confirmation and forty-four for First Communion. The local media heard about it and asked if they could do a story. Yes, of course. They requested names to interview. I informed them they could come and talk to any family who wished to talk to them, and then they could report whatever was discussed.

I'll never forget the reporter's reply.

"I can't do that. My boss wants me to connect it all up with their crimes."

I said, "What crimes?"

"You know, their cheating old women, etc."

I said, "I am from Ireland. Am I responsible also for crimes committed by other Irishmen?"

So I refused to allow the reporter on the property.

I thank the day God put me in touch with the Irish Traveller community. My priesthood has been blessed, and I pray I have been a blessing to some of them.

Do not let your hearts be troubled. You have faith in God; have faith also in me. In my Father's house there are many dwelling places. If there were not, would I have told you that I am going to prepare a place for you?

—John 14:1–2

CHAPTER 9

REST IN PEACE

All services and events surrounding the passing from this life of a loved one are filled with possibilities of God speaking to us. I often tell people that funerals are one of the great highlights of my job as a priest. I am not at all saying they are easy. Indeed, the circumstances of some funerals are extremely difficult to deal with, even with God's presence and help.

But we always call this to mind: "As our reason to have hope the favors of the Lord are not forgotten; His miracles are not spent" (Lamentations 3:21–22). God is our Father! He is a wonderful Father. He is a loving Father. He is a merciful Father. All of us are His children. Think about it! How could a loving, gentle, merciful Father not take care of His children?

Through His Son, Jesus, and the sacrifice of Jesus on the cross, He invites all His children into the fullness of His kingdom at the banquet hall of heaven. He does not force. He invites. And how could a loving, merciful Father ever reject any one of His children who come to Him? Impossible! Even if that child is a notorious sinner, the Father still welcomes him as long as that person is accepting the Father's invitation.

God's holy Word consoles us: "The souls of the just are in the hand of God and no torment shall touch them" (Wisdom 3:1). That is the good news for all families and friends whose loved one has passed on. We have not lost a loved one; the loved one is on his or her way to the Father. He or she has not arrived despite all the nice words we hear at the funeral mass or grave services, such as, "He is now with his mom and dad, his spouse, etc. in heaven."

Jesus on the cross could truly say, "It is finished. I have finished the work the Father gave me to do" (John 19:29). How many of us will be able to truthfully say, "I have finished the work my Father gave me to do?" I would safely say not too many of us will be able to say that. Maybe a few. Jesus's mother could say it, as well as some innocent souls who never reached the age of reason.

But this is not a worry. Our sins are forgiven as long as we have repented. That's where God's bountiful mercy comes in. But God is also a just god, and that is a good thing for us. Like any good dad (or mom), He holds us accountable. In any family where children are not held accountable, they never grow up. We are all too well aware of that. God forgives my sin of stealing, but He, in justice, requires me to make restitution. This is sound Catholic teaching.

Many other religions say that when God forgives, all is wiped out, even the responsibility due to sin. If that were true, there would be no need to pray for the dead that they may be loosed from their sins and the responsibilities due to sin (Maccabees 12:46). The souls of the just are in the hands of God but are not necessarily already in heaven. If they are already in heaven, we would not need to offer mass for them or pray for them or do charitable works in their name.

But we all do. We need to pray for them. They are not in torment (book of Wisdom), but we can still pray with them and for them as they complete their journey. We were there with them and for them while they were here in the flesh. That has not changed, except that they are not visibly present to us.

In everyday life, there are a whole lot of distractions. God has a difficult time competing with all those distractions. But when it comes to funeral services, it is so much easier for us to focus on God on our journey back to God and where we presently are in that journey.

At the funeral service, we give thanks to God for the blessing of our departed loved one, and we pray for him as he goes on his way to complete the journey to the banquet hall of heaven. But we also should find it much easier to focus on our own journey to God. As it says on 2 Corinthians 5:9, "We shall all have to appear before the judgment seat of Christ."

Hopefully, we are inspired by the spiritual life of our departed loved one. Hopefully, we are more open than ever to let God speak to us. Every funeral service should not only be the greatest blessing to our loved one as he leaves the valley on his way to the mountaintop (Isaiah 25:6–9) but also a huge step forward in the lives of all those who are still here in the flesh, praying for the departed one.

That's why I like funerals. They are real; they are down to earth; they are easily more God-centered than any other gathering of the family or the community. We are more available to God. We are more focused on the purpose of our earthly journeys. We are more open to allow God to do His thing.

For where two or three are gathered together in my name, there I am in the midst of them.

—Matthew 18:20

CHAPTER 10

AS HE PASSES BY

If we are tuned in, we will see God in various events and people as we pass along the journey of life. We do not have to do anything. We do not have to say anything. We just have to be fully present and aware of God in action.

Through the eyes of faith, we can easily see God making Himself known. It may be through the faith of another person in action with Christ. It may be through a person in deep prayer before the Lord. It may be through the inspirational gathering of God's people uplifted in prayer. It may be through the quiet observance of a Good Samaritan–type person helping an outcast.

Here are a few of those "God in action" type of memories that stick in my mind.

1. In my first visit to Our Lady of Lourdes Grotto, Lourdes, France, I was fully taken in by a group of French women with both hands openly raised high to God, faces emotionless, praying in unison, "Je vous salue Marie, pleine de grace." I knew no French, but before long, I was praying the Hail Mary with them in French and kept on praying it in French on my own for some months after that.
2. I happened to answer the church phone one afternoon while at St. Joseph's in Lakeland. A lady with a foreign

accent asked what time daily mass was. I told her we had two daily masses—at 7:45 a.m. and 5:30 p.m.

"Oh," she said, "I can still make the 5:30 p.m. mass. I am at the Holiday Inn."

I told her the Holiday Inn was only three miles away, a short ride in a taxi, but she went on to say she was walking. At mass that day, an older woman in baggy clothes came up for Communion. She came around to the rectory door after mass and introduced herself.

"I am Maria von Trapp. I am here in town for a symposium at Florida Southern College tomorrow. I'll see you at morning mass."

She came around for a cup of tea and light breakfast after mass. To this day, I marvel at the simple, sincere, and old-fashioned faith life that so obviously came through her conversation at breakfast. God was obviously alive in her. She obviously was not worried in the least about her image or about how others would see her. She was letting God talk through her.

I hoped and prayed that at the symposium in Florida Southern College later that morning, the students would not miss God in action through His instrument: Maria von Trapp.

3. During the 1975 Holy Year, we were blessed to be able to get Bishop Fulton Sheen to Lakeland to give an ecumenical talk to four thousand to five thousand people at the Lakeland Civic Center. There were nine or ten pastors present onstage from the different major religions in the area.

   I picked up Bishop Sheen from Tampa Airport the night before. When we arrived at the rectory, there were three young adult women waiting to meet him at 10:00 p.m. They had hitchhiked from North Florida just to meet him. Bishop Sheen took plenty of time to talk to them while I stood at a distance, gave each a scapular or medal, and obviously made their day a blessing.

Bishop Sheen presided over one English mass and preached the homily at three other English masses before his advertised big talk at the civic center. With the same Word of God at each mass, he preached four totally different homilies and then captured the audience and the pastors onstage with his spirit-filled talk on Christ's prayer for unity among Christians. I was inspired, and it seemed, so was everyone else.

But you know, what inspired me the most was Bishop Sheen taking the time late at night to bring God's presence to three young adult women.

4. Most every county in Florida has farmworkers. In the 1970s, big efforts were being made to convince their employees and farm owners to raise the hourly wage since it was so low and next to impossible to live on. One man in particular, Cesar Chavez, was the object of hate and violent threats, because he went from place to place to organize the workers and give them a platform to speak up for themselves.

    He spearheaded the United Farm Workers of America. His life was constantly in danger. He always had bodyguards around him. He never stayed in motels. I was asked to secretly put him up overnight in our rectory. I had no problem agreeing. A few of his bodyguards stayed outside on watch, and a few more inside.

    Where I saw God in action was in one of his bodyguards who spoke English well and talked freely to me about his mission from God to uplift the much-abused farmworkers. He was fully convinced that the most fruitful way he could do that was to help Cesar Chavez carry on his work in the safest possible environment, and he totally convinced me too that God was fully active in his life's work.

5. Blessed Trinity has an ongoing special missionary relationship with Our Lady of Mt. Carmel, Benque, Belize. Benque is on the border of Guatemala. Father John McHugh was a pastor there and also pastor of a separate parish across the

border in Melchor. We helped Father John build a little mission village church about an hour's drive into Guatemala.

During my first visit to Our Lady of Mt. Carmel, Father John and I and a seminarian drove out in his pickup truck to visit and bless the new little village church. While there, mixing with the people, a child of about eight climbed up high in a tree. He lost his grip and fell down about twenty feet and split his forehead open.

Father John put the mom and her injured son in the front seat of his pickup truck. He had her hold his split forehead, holding the skin together while blood flowed freely. The seminarian and I went into the back of the pickup. Father John took off with great speed to the hospital one hour away in Melchor.

On the way, while rounding an intersection, he barely slowed down to pick up a hitchhiker, who jumped into the back with us. Father John, via his little phone, had already alerted the nuns in Melchor's hospital. They were out to meet us and take the child in, and in no time, they stitched his forehead back together.

My only and immediate reaction was that I saw God in action big-time that day through the faith and quick action of Father John McHugh.

6. For over twenty-nine years now, we have had a twenty-four-hour adoration chapel at Blessed Trinity. Initially, I used to commit to one-hour adoration at midnight at the end of my day off, but I was unable to be ready for work by the time morning mass came. So I rarely went into the adoration chapel late at night, except when a rare call came in from the hospital to bring Communion to the dying.

   I got such a call after 3:00 a.m. one night. What I saw when I went into the adoration chapel is still vividly in my mind. A young mom and dad were obviously engrossed in private prayer. Their two children, one a baby and the other about two years old, were wrapped up in their blankets, asleep on the floor beside them. What a beautiful, God-centered scene.

Those two parents were not only strengthening their marriage vows, but also, they were obviously bringing their children up in a very deep-faith environment. Later on, I thought, *I should have publicly made a lot more out of this young family's faith in action.*

7. Our sister parish in Uganda also wanted a twenty-four-hour adoration chapel. For years, we used one room at their convent that also had an outside entrance. Then a few years ago, we were able to help them build a beautiful adoration chapel on the site of where their original stick/mud chapel had been for years.

   During my annual visits to our sister parish, I get up before dawn and spend some time in their adoration chapel, mostly praying the Divine Office. There are no pews or chairs in their chapel, except for one or two chairs for an old person like me to sit on.

   There are thirty-two subparishes (villages) in our sister parish. Each subparish is committed to have their members in prayer for one fixed day of each month. Between forty and one hundred members from their subparish come for adoration on that fixed day. They walk for miles. Each night, they come before dark and stay the whole night. It is not safe to travel after dark.

   When I get there in the morning, there are anywhere from five to eight families spread out over the floor. They have their little kids with them, usually asleep under bed-spreads or blankets. It is only when dawn arrives and new people show up that I begin to see just how many people had been there all night long. They are all barefoot. They all leave their shoes outside the door, except me!

   Then at dawn, the students noiselessly start streaming in. They prostrate themselves on the floor, kiss the ground, and kneel motionless in prayer. If I am praying the Divine Office with the help of a flashlight, I glance up from time to time, and the chapel has somehow filled up with fifty or sixty bodies on the floor, and I never hear them come in. Their awareness of the Lord's presence is so obvious and so natural. I'd love to take a secret video of the whole scene and show it to our students here in the US.

8. I have had the great privilege of officiating at countless funeral masses. With the help of many volunteers, the music, the hymns, the readings, the symbols, and the meal afterward are all planned ahead. Many obvious blessings come through. The family of the deceased is always given the option of providing readers for the scripture passages and the petitions.

   Once, I had a funeral mass for an Italian man. His family said they were too distraught, and no one from the family would be volunteering. That was no problem. We could always find readers. As I was about to bless the remains in the casket at the entrance to the church with the family all around the casket, I noticed a teenager close by me. She was a granddaughter.

   I don't know why I asked her if she would like to read one of the scripture passages, but she said she would love to. I gave her a moment to look it over. She proclaimed it without hesitation to the amazement of her family.

   After the mass and every time I've met her since, she never stops thanking me for allowing her a special part in her grandpa's funeral. She is now in her forties and living out of state but still happy about her special blessings.

   I often wonder how many special blessings I have missed along the way because I didn't offer the invitation.

9. Every human life is sacred. Each one is created by God. Each life is unique, each life beginning at the first moment of conception in its mother's womb. I have never yet met a lady who has had an abortion and believes it is morally right to do so because of her rational thinking.

   I met a street prostitute once in prison. We had one hour for confessions and mass, so I would tell the female inmates to keep their confessions short, one sentence per sin.

The prostitute came in and said, "You don't have time for all my sins. I have broken all the commandments, except the fifth."

I don't know why I said it, but I remarked, "So you never had an abortion?"

"Oh," she said, "is that the fifth? I have had eight abortions!"

I said, "You came out with that number very fast."

She said, "I remember every one of them like it was yesterday. They all still bother me."

She was so happy she could get forgiveness for all her abortions and could now start a fresh life.

God can be active anywhere, anytime, and under any kind of unusual circumstances. We need to give Him the opportunity.

10. Over the years, I have been blessed to be there for various addicts in their recovery journeys. One addict who has been faithful in his recovery program for over thirty years spends a good part of his life helping other addicts to get into recovery, especially through the twelve-step movement.

    He invited me to give a talk at a closed twelve-step meeting that had fifty to sixty addicts present. Normally, to give a talk to them, you had to be a recovering addict yourself, but they made an exception for me. I did not know if my talk was helpful or not to them. They were all very polite and very friendly to me.

    What struck me the most was the rest of the meeting and their questions. They were all on the same level—no big shots and no inferiors. All were there with a common mission: to admit that their addiction was beyond their control, that they had God or a higher power to submit to, and that they needed one another to stay on the road to recovery and a normal life.

God was obviously and truly at work in and through that whole gathering of addicts. I have often thought—and so have many others—that a similar type of gathering would be a great blessing and an opportunity for us to grow together in our faith journeys. We have everything in common with addicts. It is just that we have not been exposed.

11. George died in his thirties. His Hispanic mother was in prison at the time and was not allowed to be present at her son's funeral mass. She then became very bitter and turned angry toward God. She still encouraged her other children and grandchildren to keep up their Catholic faith lives, but she herself had stopped praying and did not go to mass in prison. But somehow, she was there for mass on one of my visits.

    While waiting for the other inmates to arrive, I began a conversation with her. Reluctantly, she revealed her story. I told her we had no special intention for this mass, and we could say it for her and her family and for George (RIP). Her face began to light up. She went to confession, and she received Communion.

    After mass, she said to me, "I have to light a candle for my son."

    That was not possible in prison, but I told her that since I was going back to church, I would light her candle and one for my recently deceased brother and one for her and her family.

    Isn't it amazing how simple it can be to help God bring someone back to Him and His church?

I conclude this chapter by reminding myself, I wish I were more fully awake and present to observe God as He passes by in all the ordinary and sometimes not-so-ordinary events of life.

Section III

Remaining on Course

If you are willing to listen, you will learn; if you apply yourself, you will be shrewd.

—Sirach 6:33

Chapter 11

Stand There!

After a blistering-hot celebration of my first mass in the US at the outdoor shrine of Nombre de Dios in St. Augustine, I was assigned to Father Joe Barry, Resurrection Catholic Church, Jacksonville. Showing me around the parish facilities, Father Barry brought me to the front doors, the only entrance to the church. He had me stand in the middle in front of the doors.

He said, "Stand there! Don't move right or left. Let the people go by you into the church."

I was obedient, so I did it. I noticed he never did.

Each Sunday before every mass, I arrived half an hour early. I stood there, and in my own fumbling way, I greeted each one entering church. Me with my unfamiliar Irish accent and they with their Southern drawl greeted one another. They did not understand me, and I did not understand them. But being the obedient young priest that I was, I stuck it out! We got used to one another.

After three months of sweating it out, I got to love standing at the front door before every mass. In my fifty-six years as a priest, I concluded long ago that it was a big *God thing* for Father Barry to put me at the front door.

Lots and lots of blessings happen at the front door. People get used to you and relax. You get used to them. They have questions they wouldn't otherwise ask. They have stories to tell. They have prayer requests. They have objects to bless. They request house blessings. They have requests for a hospital or house visit for a sick member of the family.

It does add work to a priest's daily life, but for me, it also saves me a lot of work. I find new witness speakers by being at the door, and I fill volunteer ministry positions: "Hey, Joe, would you like to serve on the Brother's Keeper Board or the Stewardship Committee or the fund drive or volunteer at the front office or stuff bulletins on Friday?"

Most priests, not all, greet people after mass. That is great, but most people are gone in a matter of a few minutes. Before mass, people drift in over the space of a half hour. At the time, I was not at ease when Father Barry told me to stand there, but now it would be a real sacrifice for me if I did not stand there. For three hours each weekend, one-half hour before six English masses, I now sit on a four-foot barstool to greet people. At age eighty-one, it is too much on my feet to stand there, but it would be, for me, against God's will not to be there.

People will at times attempt to draw me away from the door to do things like put oil in the candles or paper in the restrooms, hear a confession, etc. I do my best not to move away from the door, even for the one who wants confession! I usually try to get them to see me after mass when the people are gone. Most do not. They seem to want a quick confession. But if it is obvious they are coming back to mass, then by all means, I take a good break from the door.

I have known for years and years that spending time at the church door before mass is a very fruitful spiritual time for me and the community. My prayer would be that priests give it an honest test.

My soul proclaims the greatness of the Lord; my spirit rejoices in God my savior.

—Luke 1:46–48

CHAPTER 12

HAIL MARY

When we were growing up, family prayer was no big deal. Everyone, as far as we knew, prayed as a family seven nights a week. The rosary was the normal family prayer. In our house, Mom led the rosary. Dad led the first decade, Mom led the second decade, and three of us twelve kids led the next three decades going from oldest to youngest. So every fourth night, you got to lead a decade of the rosary.

Then when there was a special need, such as a serious sickness somewhere in the family, Mom added prayers to the rosary. Even when that need had passed, we continued praying those extra prayers. Another need came up and we added more prayers. In time, no one remembered what the original need was for the added prayers. That's why the joke goes that the trimmings of the rosary are often longer than the rosary.

For a time in the late sixties and seventies, when word was out that your work was your prayer, I was careless with getting the rosary prayed daily. I got all that corrected in a big way on my first pilgrimage to Medjugorje in 1989.

I got in the habit of praying the rosary while I drive. Most every day, I drive somewhere, so it is no problem at all to pray at least one rosary. The rosary is like a mantra for me. It puts me in God's presence, and I don't necessarily have to dwell on the words. Holy thoughts float into my mind while praying the rosary. I prefer to turn off radio and tapes and be quiet so God can get through more easily. While on long journeys, I have a plan to pray the rosary every fifty miles. You'll be surprised how short journeys become!

I encourage families to pray as a family. I don't think it is catching on too well. Why did praying as a family ever stop? If not the rosary, then it must be some other family prayer in its place. Kids who are coached in and pray the rosary, at least one decade, have no trouble praying it. You give each child a lead part as often as possible.

In place of the rosary, a simple family prayer that flows without any preplanning each evening would suffice. Start with any prayer—the Lord's Prayer, for example. Have one person read a short passage of scripture following from the passage read the night before, then pause for two minutes. (Use an egg timer!) During the pause, reflect on the scripture and on your day (no discussion).

Follow with an Act of Contrition together and conclude with a prayer or hymn to Mary, such as Hail, Holy Queen, the Memorare, or a Hail Mary. Then Dad or whoever is the head that evening gives a simple blessing over the family.

Where there are children, the best time for family prayer is just before the youngest child goes to bed. And yes, make it a must that all members living in the house, if at all possible, be present for prayer.

We all need to set a prayer time. We all need to cultivate the art of silence. God wants to get through, but it is next to impossible for Him without an opening.

As you know, we treated each one of you as a father treats his children, exhorting and encouraging you and insisting that you conduct yourselves as worthy of the God who calls you into his kingdom and glory.

—1 Thessalonians 2:11

Chapter 13

Just Call Me Father

Over the years, the Catholic church has added many, many titles not found in the Bible. Followers of Christ were called Christians first at Antioch (Acts 11:26), so that title is in the Bible. The title presbyter (priest) is very much in the Bible. The title deacon is in the Bible. The deacon Stephen was the first to die for Christ. The title apostle (or bishop) is clearly in the Bible. The title papa or pope is very much in the Bible.

All the other titles, such as cardinal, canon, monsignor, dean, reverend, very reverend, papal delegate, etc., came into being as the church spread all over the world and got organized. Some of the titles are necessary, and maybe some have been overused.

The one title that I've always seen as fully meaningful and a challenge is the title father. To be a mom or a dad is a great privilege but also a huge challenge. To be a father, a spiritual father of a community, is a big privilege and a mighty challenge. It is a never-ending challenge.

The spiritual needs of the entire community are so varied, so individual, so complicated at times, so much in process, often so misunderstood, that the father must always be on his toes, seeking a clearer understanding from God as to which is the best way to serve. But also, the effort put into being a father is rewarded a thousandfold in countless ways.

When you are a father, you are never off work, even on your free day. If you can succeed in turning off being a father, then maybe this is just a job and not so much a calling. I sometimes tell people I have a full-time hobby and no real work.

A few years ago, I reluctantly accepted the title monsignor. Yes, it was an honor, but it made me most uncomfortable. It didn't describe me. I have more or less succeeded in getting people to refer to me by the very meaningful and challenging title Father Pat, except for a few people in the chancery office.

As the years go by, the challenge of being a spiritual father has grown by leaps and bounds. I'm happy with the challenge. Like old Canon Galvin in Aylesbury, England, I can easily see that advanced age is not a reason to pull back from being a father. The only thing that would make me pull back would be deteriorating health.

So far, God must know that I could much more easily cope with good health while doing full-time in the mission than having very poor health in a retirement home. But then again, if that happens, God would give me the grace to deal with it in a Christian way.

Do whatever He tells you.

—John 2:5

Chapter 14

When God Finds You

Many say you can find God anywhere, or God can find you anywhere if you allow Him to. You can be at work or driving your car or visiting your family or praying in church, and God is readily available to you.

But all things being more or less equal, it is much easier to find God or for God to find you when you are visiting a holy shrine that has a lot of proven evidence of God in action. I have found this to be especially true for me over the years.

In my visits to Knock, Ireland (annual), Lough Derg, Ireland (annual), the Holy Land (three times), Fatima (once), Lourdes (twice), and Medjugorje (about ten times), I have found it much easier than usual to stay in God's presence and let Him speak to me.

I would like to elaborate a little on two of those places of pilgrimage.

Lourdes. My first visit there was with my brother and sister and our aunt Angela, who paid for the trip. We were in our early twenties. In Lourdes, every day, there are two major processions, apart from exposition, holy hours, and the celebration of mass.

One procession, around midday, includes all the sick in walkers, wheelchairs, stretchers, etc. The other is in the evening, and it is a torchlight procession. Now sixty years later, I am still uplifted by memories of the spiritual awareness of God's love and presence so obvious in those processions.

I returned to Lourdes in the seventies with a group from the US. We lined up for the midday procession of the sick. Usually, you filed in behind the flag of your country. But since there was no US flag in line, we lined up behind the Irish flag. Beside me were two grandmothers, a young mom, and her ten-month-old baby James.

Baby James was declared by his doctor blind from birth. The two grandmothers had faith; the young mom did not. The two grandmothers persuaded the young mom to leave their home in England, travel by land, cross by boat to France, and travel by land to Lourdes near the border of Spain. They made no prior plans. They had just arrived when I met them. The young mom was mostly negative about this seemingly wasted, long, arduous journey.

Most all people went to the male or female baths each day in Lourdes, where they stripped off, got fully dipped in the miraculous Lourdes water, and said the printed prayer while in the water. They came out, dried off with a wet towel used by the person before them, and put their clothes back on. I had trouble convincing my US group to do this. Eventually, almost all of them did.

But the young mom initially told me, "No way. Why would I subject my child to this?"

I remember the story from 2 Kings 5 of Naaman and his group who came down to Elisha, the prophet in Israel, seeking a healing. The prophet didn't even come out to meet him but gave him instructions to dip himself seven times in the waters of the Jordan.

He got insulted, saying, "Don't I have water back home to dip in?"

But his companions persuaded him to just do it since he was already here. He did, and lo and behold, he was healed. I told this story to the young mom and convinced her to dip her baby, James, in the Lourdes water.

For three days in a row, we met in the procession. Each day, she dipped her son in the water. She even dipped herself. By the third day, she was trying to convince us that there was something happening to James's eyes. We could not see anything. We exchanged addresses, and she returned to England.

She went to the baby's doctor and tried to convince the doctor a change was taking place in James's eyes. The doctor persuaded her that it was impossible, that he was physically missing a part, and therefore, he would never see.

The next time she wrote back to me, she included an article from an English newspaper with a large photo of baby James and herself, and the title read "Miracle Baby James!" I wrote back to congratulate her. My letter was returned—"Moved. No forwarding address."

I often wonder if the young mother has gotten back her faith. James would be about forty now. Is he a faith-filled man?

My second story on Lourdes involves a young man named Jason, twenty years old, who had an inoperable brain tumor. He was one of about ten children. His parents were poor. Our parish decided to give Jason and his parents a free trip to Lourdes before Jason passed on. Jason's mom expected a miracle despite all the counsel we gave her not to put her whole faith on a miracle.

They had a great pilgrimage. Jason came back and died a short time later, but the mother brought back Lourdes water and claimed a miracle had taken place with a neighbor she had given the water to. She wrote down all the details in a booklet called *The Miracle of Jason*. It wasn't written well, so she couldn't get it published, but she somehow got it to the Catholic Truth Society, a publishing company in England. They cleaned up the English and got it ready and published it. The pamphlet *The Miracle of Jason* was placed among dozens of other pamphlets in the pamphlet racks at the entrances of Catholic churches in England.

A lady who had been away from the practice of her faith in England was driving along, and while passing a Catholic church, she got the urge to go in for a visit. On the way in, she looked at the pamphlet rack, and the only pamphlet that caught her attention was *The Miracle of Jason*. She wrote to me because my name and my parish were listed in the introduction of the pamphlet. She told me that *The Miracle of Jason* got her fully back into being a happy, active Catholic. To me, her full return to the Catholic faith was a much greater miracle than if Jason's tumor had been healed.

Medjugorje. While home on holiday in Ireland in 1989, my mom and my sister, Concepta, asked me if I would join them on a pilgrimage to Medjugorje in Bosnia, Herzegovina. There was just one available seat left on the charter flight from Dublin to Mostar. I knew little or nothing about all the happenings in Medjugorje since 1981, but I went.

It was a powerful spiritual pilgrimage. My sister and I climbed up Mount Krizevac, praying the stations of the cross on the way up. We asked our mom not to go since she was eighty!

While we were on the way, she met another old woman, who said to her, "Don't pay any attention to those young people. You and I can do it on our own."

They did without a mishap.

We all climbed the smaller apparition hill known as Podbrdo, praying the Joyful Mysteries of the rosary on the way up and the Sorrowful Mysteries around the top, stopping for prayer at the place of the apparitions, and praying the Glorious Mysteries on the way down. It was all too obvious that Mary, the mother of Jesus, was present and working in the crowds, thousands of people who had come from all over the world.

Lines of people, all speaking different languages, were waiting to go to confession outside, where there were twenty-five or more outdoor confession boxes or just priests sitting on a chair with a penitent in a chair beside them. I still remember the first confession I made in Medjugorje and the challenging penance the priest gave me, which has been a big blessing to me down to this day.

Two years later, I came back with a group from the US. I am not a good tourist, so I challenged our travel agent to fly us to Mostar and not to the tourist town of Dubrovnik, which was over three hours by bus from Medjugorje. Mostar was only forty-five minutes away. The agent said it wasn't possible.

The first morning in Medjugorje, I was walking up to St. James Church for the English mass when I noticed a small travel agency office. I asked the young agent, Dijana, who was new on the job and had broken English, if there were any flights from Mostar to Zagreb.

She gave me a list of several flights a day coming and going from Mostar to Zagreb.

Later that same day, I was walking back up to church at 5:30 p.m. for the 6:00 p.m. Croatian mass and apparition. The travel agency office had closed at 5:00 p.m., but Dijana was out there on the sidewalk, observing the crowds walking by and hoping to catch the man she had met early in the morning and had given a list of flights from Mostar to Zagreb.

She was excited to find me and apologized big-time for the list of flights she had given me and gave me a new list that was only half as long. But she included a card with her full name and address. I was impressed. I sent her a thank-you note when I got to Ireland.

That was thirty years ago. Since then, I got a full account by her from the war that broke up former Yugoslavia into six independent countries. Dijana's boyfriend, Miro, was in that war, as was her brother Dragan. Dijana and Miro got married during the war. They fled to Germany as refugees during the war. I was able to give her a good reference for a job in a German hotel where I knew an Irish employer.

When the war was over, they were not allowed to stay in Germany. Back home in Apollo, near Mostar, they had very little to live on and had to live with Miro's parents. They got a site for a house from Miro's dad with no possibility of building their own home. I convinced them to get a plan and round up Miro's friends to do the building as volunteers, and I would see to it they got the money for all the materials. It turned out to be a beautiful home.

I have been to Medjugorje every second year since the late nineties. Our group stops each year at Miro and Dijana's home and their two kids. We have an English/Croatian mass and dinner afterward, a highlight of our visit to Medjugorje.

On my third visit back to Medjugorje, my first visit to their new home, Dijana's brother had made several nice rosaries from local materials. He had concocted a little electric gadget to break the local stones into beads and another gadget to make holes in each bead for the wire. His kids had formed an assembly line to put the beads together.

I was impressed, and I asked him why he didn't go into business selling rosaries. He said the Turkish women could produce rosaries far cheaper, so it would not be worth all his work. I told him we had a shop back in our parish, and I could sell them there for ten dollars. It cost one dollar for the materials. We did this for years, selling thousands of his homemade rosaries, and with the money, he was able to send his children to university.

We have many other similar stories involving this Croatian family, but you get the picture. All this happened because one young lady, Dijana, new on the job, made a mistake and went way out of her way, standing on the side of a road for a half hour, hoping to correct her mistake. See what God can do when you go out of your way to put things right?

The light shines in the darkness and the darkness has not overcome it.

—John 1:5

CHAPTER 15

WHEN THE LIGHTS GO OUT

During my recent five-day mission trip to our sister parish, Blessed Trinity, Nalweyo, Uganda, I was at my usual spot between 5:30 a.m. and 6:30 a.m., praying the Divine Office, when the lights went out. That was not unusual there. They had had electricity in that area for only a few years. Most areas as yet did not.

I liked to go into the adoration chapel primarily to do my own prayer and meditation early morning. But I was also drawn there, inspired by the many people who had spent the night there in prayer or just sleeping and the dozens and dozens of school students, grade school and secondary, all boarders, who quietly drifted in and out, shoeless, before they headed for breakfast and class.

My hour in the adoration chapel usually had a neat plan. So when the lights went out while in total darkness, I asked God why He let be disturbed such an inspiring, prayerful atmosphere. He led me to all kinds of different reflections on what happened and what should be—could be—happening when our plans were disturbed or when the lights went out!

For the most part, God, through the disturbance, was giving us a wake-up call, disturbing our routine. He was asking us to dig deeper and evaluate our routine approach to life. How God-connected was it? Was it possible that this experience/disturbance could and should be turned into a real blessing?

While the lights were only out for ten or fifteen minutes, I was led to prayerfully reflect on the type of God-centered, Christian approach I would really try to bring to the seven villages whose leaders and priest we had planned to meet during that day. The lights-out reflection made a big difference. I found it much easier to be fully present to the total situation and concerns of the people in each village, and it lasted all day until the conclusion of the seventh visit. Normally, by then, I would have been worn out and more than ready to end the day. That reflective presence lasted the whole five days for all thirty-five meetings with village leaders.

I believe we get not only new spiritual vision but also extra physical energy when we make good of a hurtful setback or a disturbance in our lives. In our meetings with the people of the villages, many easily recounted the blessings brought to their families and their village because of COVID-19. They were not minimizing the hardships. It was just that they had truly grown through them and had become more trusting in God and their need to stay very much in touch with Him and more united within their families.

The lights came on, and life returned to normal. Or did it? One man was still snoring in the presence of God. Well, didn't that happen in the garden of Gethsemane also? Another young mom succeeded in quieting her few-months-old baby by breastfeeding. The school students were still drifting in, shoeless, kissing the ground, praying bowed to the ground, rekissing the holy ground, and backing out again as quietly as they came in, retrieving their shoes and then going on their way. I bet their day was different.

I went back to where I had left off and returned to my normal routine. Or did I?

God grant me the serenity to accept the things I cannot change, courage to change the things I can, and the wisdom to know the difference.

—the Serenity Prayer

CHAPTER 16

CARRYING CROSSES—CHOSEN AND UNCHOSEN

Life is full of sacrifices. In the spiritual context, we may refer to them as crosses. Some crosses are relatively light and easy to manage. Others are downright heavy, often appearing to be unmanageable and, humanly speaking, outside our ability to cope.

It is true that many or some crosses or suffering can be avoided. We must act as Jesus did: "He went about doing good" (Acts 10:38). He uplifted people. He healed people. He did all He could to remove human suffering. So the message of the gospel is, if suffering or crosses can be avoided or remedied, we must plan ahead to remove the cross.

Good students plan ahead and study hard in order to avoid the cross or pain of a poor grade or the disappointment of their parents. Healthy-minded people check in with their doctors at the beginning of a medical problem in order to avoid the serious possible problems caused by the neglect of early warnings.

Joseph, Jacob's eleventh son, got Egypt to plan ahead and make wise use of the seven years of plenty and thereby saved the Egyptians from starvation during the seven years of drought. We change out our growing-bald car tires to avoid the possible crash from a sudden flat tire.

But many sufferings are unavoidable and have to be endured. We don't cause them. They are thrust upon us. They are part of our life. There is no way around them. We can resent them and blame others for them. Or we can even deny the suffering is happening, such as when the aging process is obviously setting in.

We can curse the suffering and grow hard of heart, or we can decide to accept and endure the unavoidable suffering with patience. We can even go one step further and grow in character and faith by the way we handle the suffering.

Good Christians are inspired by the way in which Jesus handled His sufferings. In Mark 13:13, He said, "The one who endures to the end will be saved." In the garden of Gethsemane, we hear how He wished to avoid the suffering of the passion if that were possible.

For us too, we try to move from reluctance and negativity to quiet, prayerful acceptance; and in the process of quiet acceptance, God can speak to us. If we reach this stage of quiet, prayerful acceptance, it always means there is great love involved. That great love can be for an ailing spouse or for a child or for the church or for the country or something a job requires you to fight for, etc.

Recently, I officiated at the funeral mass of a young man. For thirty years, he showed little love or concern for his faith, his family, his friends, and life in general. He seemed to have lived a selfish, carefree life with very little concern for others. Then he got diagnosed with cancer and was given just a few months to live.

He was sent as a patient to a cancer treatment center. There he was immediately exposed to the loving personal care of just about all the employees at the center. The light bulb came on in his head. The personal care of others inspired him to make an about-face in life. He became interested in the well-being of the other patients he was exposed to. Others talked about their faith and how Jesus dealt with suffering.

This young man got all caught up in Christ's life and message. Every opportunity given to him, he talked about his newfound faith. He engaged others in the faith journey. He inspired many people with the way he dealt with his own cancer. He actually outlived all the medical predictions of his approaching death by seven and a half years. He readily admitted he was thankful to God for his cross of cancer, because it led him to a whole new, inspiring, and meaningful seven and a half extra years.

So God, if allowed, can speak to us through the sufferings thrust upon us! But God can more easily and more readily speak to us when we actually go out of our way and choose a cross that is not part of our normal responsibility. We can choose to shop for a sick neighbor each week or tutor a weak student or work in the soup kitchen or go on a mission trip or sit at a table and register new voters or go on a retreat or work for Habitat for Humanity or visit the sick, etc.

Why can God more easily speak to us when we volunteer to accept a cross? Because we are already receptive to Him. We don't have to go through a process of reflecting and striving to reach a conclusion about why we are doing what we have chosen to do. We are in the right frame of mind; we are already listening. We are open.

If you take an honest look at your life, you will easily conclude that many of your God-inspired moments or ideas came to you when you were going out of your way to help a situation. We all need to thank God for inspiring us to go the extra mile. It is then that we are more easily available to Him. They say that true Christianity only begins with what we voluntarily take on for Christ over and above carrying out the obligations entrusted upon us.

Section IV

The Need to Give

All shall give as they are able, according to the blessings of the Lord your God, has bestowed on you.

—Deuteronomy 16:17

CHAPTER 17

STEWARDSHIP: GOD IS NUMBER ONE

After I had been a year or two at Blessed Trinity, Ocala, during a parish council meeting, the topic of how much financial support the parish should give to our Catholic grade school became controversial. At the time, the parish was helping the school budget with a little over two thousand dollars a week. For some on the council, that was too much.

One member related how he had seen a parish video on stewardship from St. Francis of Assisi in Wichita, Kansas. The video clearly put the mass at the high point of our Catholic faith, and everything, every ministry, flowed from that, including finances. To break the stalemate in our discussion, I asked that we hold off on our decision and first watch the video.

When we all watched the stewardship video, we were convinced as a council that our parish needed to pursue the St. Francis of Assisi parish model. Deacon Vernon Krajewski and I went to Wichita, Kansas, for three days. We came back 100 percent convinced that Blessed Trinity Parish needed to pursue the total Stewardship Way of Life, including a perpetual adoration chapel.

Again, it was all too obvious that God was handing us a plan of Christian action for the entire parish. The plan suited every person and family. It put every ministry in a proper relationship with God, who was the only source of all our blessings. We owed Him a big and continuous thank-you!

That is why the mass, the Eucharist, which means thanksgiving, is the high point of the Stewardship Way of Life. We are all blessed. We all have gifts. We learn as we go what our gifts are, so our return of thanks to God has to increase as we get to more fully know our gifts from Him.

We are responsible for these gifts. Gifts need to be developed. They need to be used—not for selfish gain or greed but for the well-being of others and for the promotion of the kingdom of God. That spirituality—God is the giver, and we are the receivers, and we need to make a fitting return to God—flows easily from all of Scripture.

Look at the parables of the sower (Matthew 13:1–23), the mustard seed (Matthew 13:22–43), the rich man and Lazarus (Luke 16:19–31), the story (conversion) of Zacchaeus (Luke 19:1–10), the talents (Matthew 25:14–31), the fig tree (Luke 13:6–9), the Good Samaritan (Luke 10:25–37), etc. The spirituality of the Stewardship Way of Life is a perfect fit for and flows from Jesus's life, His teachings, His parables, and His clear message to nonstewardship people, who would be left out of the kingdom.

While we always had many aspects of stewardship in our parish prior to our visit to Wichita, there was no real bonding between all the ministries and projects and volunteers unifying them all under the great master plan that God had given us under the Stewardship Way of Life. Now no matter what ministry or Christian work a person is involved in, he or she can easily see how it flows from God, who has given us the gifts to make a return to benefit His spiritual kingdom on earth.

Even our children, after hearing about the Stewardship Way of Life since they were in preschool, believe that stewardship is the only way. They find it very easy to accept that God is a most generous and free giver. They see it as normal to give back a meaningful gift to God.

At all school masses, each one of them has prepared a gift for God. While a few may include money, most are going to help out at home without being asked, or they are going to pick up trash, or they are going to use their talents to help their teacher or classmates. Our children assume that every parish uses the stewardship language they are familiar with.

Once a family pledges in writing to follow the Stewardship Way of Life, then all ministries of the parish are free! No fees are charged, not even tuition for the Catholic grade school and Catholic high school. All families on the Stewardship Way of Life can send their children to the Catholic school even if they are below the poverty line.

This works. It has worked for twenty-nine years. It has worked through down economies and growing economies. The other big result of this way of life is that our Catholic grade school's student population has tripled in size, and 60 percent of the local Catholic high school families do not pay tuition. Also, families give God not only their first fruits in money; many of them also give God a tithe of their year-end bonus and also a tithe of their profit when they sell a business or a residence.

While money is involved, it is not primarily about the money. As one of our outspoken Christians often says, "It is not about the money, dummy!" Those who are very much into the spirituality of the Stewardship Way of Life know it is never primarily about the money. It is about recognizing God as the sole giver.

We have the use of those gifts. We are tenants, not owners. We develop them and make a fitting response in accordance to the gifts and opportunities available to us. That makes for a more fulfilling, less anxious, and happy way of life, even here on earth, with a promise by Jesus of a hundredfold return in the next.

Many priests seem very hesitant about taking on the full spirituality of stewardship. I say many, but I really do not know the number. The conversations I have still tend to revolve around the money and not about God, the owner, who has gifted us and has asked us to give an accounting of our whole lives, not just money.

He, God, wants us to be in the right relationship with Him. When we try it His way, money has no real hold on us. Money will never be our first or biggest worry. We will be very free to give God back His share, His due.

So, you could not keep watch with me for one hour?

—Matthew 26:40

CHAPTER 18

WATCH AND PRAY

During our three-day visit to St. Francis of Assisi, Wichita, we made several visits to their twenty-four-hour adoration chapel. All the hours were filled with at least one committed person in prayer all twenty-four hours. Others, like us, drifted in and out for long or short periods of prayer. The deacon and I easily concluded we should put a separate twenty-four-hour adoration chapel on our parish grounds.

The parish lined up a homilist to preach on perpetual adoration at all the weekend masses, English and Spanish. Our guest homilist, Father Martin Lucia, did a very inspiring job. We passed out adoration commitment sheets at each mass. Over eight hundred initially signed up for a holy hour each week. By the time our parish adoration coordinator and her four team members got all the commitments verified, we were left with over four hundred people who also signed up to pray before the exposed Blessed Sacrament each week at a given hour.

For twenty-nine years now, twenty-four hours a day, people are in the adoration chapel before the Lord. We built our adoration chapel attached to the presbytery rectory. Priests in our house can enter from the house. All others come in through an outside door as long as they know the code. We freely give out the code to anyone and everyone who is interested in going in to talk to the Lord.

We have filled all hours with mostly two committed persons. We publish a list of substitutes to fill in for those who cannot be there on a given week. We publish vacant hours every week in the parish weekly bulletin. About 20 percent of our residents move every year, so we are always adding new commitments. Some people have kept the same hour of prayer for the last twenty-nine years. Many drop in daily but may never have a committed hour.

I drop in for reflection and for praying the Divine Office every day before the workday begins, except on my day off. Actually, I do not do any real work. I have a permanent hobby, which I enjoy more and more as the years go by. Our adoration chapel has inspired countless people in their walk with the Lord. It has been a real blessing to me in trying to live out my priesthood.

Some may call it a distraction, but I call it an inspiration when while I am praying the Breviary my mind gets flooded with thoughts of how to deal with items on the agenda that day. The Lord, in my belief, gives me new ways to look at things, new thoughts or ideas that are fresh and are easy ways forward. I get to role-play with Jesus many of the affairs of His kingdom that are on the parish agenda or new items put by Him on my mind that need to be pursued with the parishioners.

While I'm on vacation in Ireland or on a pilgrimage to Medjugorje, I find it the easiest thing in the world to pop into any available adoration chapel that is open to the public. I am not one who spends hours in prayer, but I do find that any adoration chapel is one of the great keys to helping one stay on track with the good Lord's mission for us on earth.

Much will be required of the person entrusted with much, and still more will be demanded of the person entrusted with more.

—Luke 12:48

CHAPTER 19

PUTTING GOD FIRST

The spirituality of putting God first with our time, talent, and treasure is not only a unique blessing to everyone who actually tries to live it out daily but is also and maybe more so a huge blessing to the God-given mission of the parish. A big portion of what the parish has been able to attempt and accomplish comes about through people sharing their time, talents, and treasure over and above their weekly mass offerings.

For over twenty-five years, we did not buy a bucket of paint even though we built over twenty new buildings and painted all buildings on rotation every seventh year. One family in the parish who used to own a paint manufacturing plant supplied all the paint. We have not bought any underground pipes or outlets or manholes, because another parish family owns a concrete manufacturing plant. We have not bought any sod, because another lady, now deceased, owned a sod farm. As far as we have been allowed, we have used the free services of plumbers, electricians, painters, mechanics, carpenters, technicians, and building contractors.

We have also benefitted from the free services of RNs, doctors, dentists, teachers, deacons, tutors, counselors, attorneys, real estate agents, architects, civil engineers, finance counselors, artists, typists, volunteer front office receptionists, musicians, handymen, etc. Also, there are the hundreds of volunteers who fill all the liturgy roles, the teaching (catechists) positions, service to the poor positions, leading adult religious education positions, etc.

God made us all in such a way that it is only natural for us to do like He does—give back freely and share with others where there is a real need—and we can rightfully feel good about it and do not have a need to boast about it. The act of free giving in itself has its own built-in satisfaction. But the danger that can often happen is that we get to enjoy so much the act of giving or sharing that we can lose track of our own needs and get ourselves overextended.

The spirituality of the Stewardship Way of Life also calls us not only to share but also to take good care of the greatest gift of all that God has given us: the gift of our own precious, unique life. True stewardship calls for a good dose of both—the constant care of and building up of oneself and the regular sharing of the gift of that life when it makes good common sense. Under the umbrella of stewardship, God can get His people to do simple and mighty things. And when it is good stewardship, there is no dangerous strain on either way.

I often ask myself why it took so long for me to see and promote the full message of stewardship. When you finally get it, it is a no-brainer. As far as we are able to promote it and get people to see it and follow it, we bring joy and peace and full meaning to them. We do them a big favor. It is good news; it is biblical good news.

What we do for ourselves dies with us, what we do for others and the world remains and is immortal.

—Albert Pine

CHAPTER 20

DIVINE DIRECTION

When a disaster occurs, such as a hurricane, tornado, cyclone, or refugees fleeing from war or starvation, most all God-fearing people have no trouble giving financial aid. The problem often is that the funds donated are put into a big, big fund, and we rarely hear anymore. What happened? Who was helped? Was the money mostly used for office expenses, staffing, flight tickets, etc.?

Very few charities have a record of putting more than 80 percent of the donations received into actually helping people. The two that come to mind that have been verified spending 80 percent or more helping people are Catholic Relief Services and Food for the Poor.

We as a parish have confidence using CRS when it comes to international disaster aid. Food for the Poor has presented their charity twice over the years in our parish. There are at least five or six disaster causes that come to mind where we did not put the funds collected into a large fund. I firmly believe God was pointing the way as to where to put the funds.

When Hurricane Andrew devastated the Key West area in 1992, all parishes took up a collection. We got more than $17,000. The local paper had a lead article, with photos, declaring Habitat for Humanity a winner over Hurricane Andrew on a score of 17 to 0. All houses in the path of Andrew were destroyed or badly damaged, except for seventeen houses built by Habitat. They were intact. We sent all our money to Habitat in South Florida.

When the gulf coast, including New Orleans, was hit by Hurricane Katrina, some who lost their homes ended up in Ocala and came to our 4:00 p.m. Saturday mass. I asked one family how badly their parish church and school were hit and was told they were destroyed. They gave me a phone number for the parish.

I phoned and phoned, and finally, an Irish nun answered. I told her we had close to fifty thousand dollars for victims of the hurricane. If she got it, what would she do with it? She gave me a full and detailed answer of the help she could bring to dozens of families to get them back to some kind of a normal life. We exchanged details on how to send the money, and she promised to give a detailed accounting as to how the money was spent.

Before we hung up, she asked me, "What did you say your last name was?"

I said, "Sheedy from Clare."

"Oh," she said, "your nephew is married to my niece in Chicago."

Yes, God!

When the earthquake hit the center of Northridge, Los Angeles, we collected forty thousand dollars in our parish-wide effort. Out of curiosity, I checked the Catholic directory to see what Catholic church was there and who was the pastor in Northridge. Yes, God did it again. The pastor was Father Peter Moran, a classmate of mine. We sent him the forty thousand dollars.

When Haiti was hit by Hurricane Matthew in 2016 again, we all took up a collection, and money was to be put into a big fund in the diocese for Haiti. We got $56,000. I sent $16,000 to the big fund and looked for a hands-on project for the remaining $40,000. I could not come up with one using my local Haitian contact.

A short time later, I was making my annual three-day pilgrimage to Lough Derg in North Ireland. There are no strangers in Lough Derg. We are all fasting in bare feet with no sleep. I was talking to three RNs from Dublin. They were very enthusiastic about their work. One of them related the part-time RN work she did in Haiti on assignment. My ears perked up. Did she know of any basic needs caused by the hurricane?

She informed me of a children's hospital ward that was partially destroyed. She gave me the name and email address of a good nun in charge. Back in Florida, we made the arrangements to send the forty thousand dollars for direct repairs to the children's ward. Yes, God, You provided the answer, and we all needed to be tuned in. The only trouble with the Haitian donations was, the good nun now had our contact info, and she was not afraid to seek more help.

Recently, we asked parishioners to sponsor thirty-five-dollar solar lamps for the families of 307 students in one school up in the mountains, where they had no electricity. The solar lamps did not only provide light, but you could also use it to recharge your cell phone and play your radio. This project was concluded in a few weeks, and it cost the parish nothing.

We should always collect funds and supplies when a disaster hits. People really want to uplift the victims of disasters. The worry is if our funds are really going to go help the victims. We at Blessed Trinity were blessed in all stories above to get God's direct input on how to use the funds 100 percent for the victims.

Be faithful to small
things for it is in them
that your strength lies.
—St. Teresa of Calcutta

CHAPTER 21

GIVE-AND-TAKE

In numerous articles and books I have read, one must be good not only at giving but also at receiving. They tell me I am pretty good at receiving for God and the church.

For more than sixty years, I have always stayed in touch with people unless it is clear they have dropped me from their list. I usually get in touch, by personal letter or card, with all at least three times a year—Christmas, the obvious time, when I get to Ireland every July, and in September.

I never drop anyone from my more than 250 contacts in the US and 130 contacts overseas. Each one on the list has his or her own personal story. I do not do Facebook or text, but I will use email, especially to countries where mail delivery is unreliable, such as Uganda and Bosnia and Herzegovina. I put my personal time into communicating with my list, especially on my day off each Monday.

For about thirty years now, our parish has run a big annual raffle for our Catholic grade school. I use the occasion to mail two books of tickets (worth forty dollars) to each one on my US list. In my letter to them, as well as catching them up-to-date on my own journey, I let them know all donations I get from my mail will go 100 percent to building village schools in our sister parish in Uganda. Nothing stays in the US.

People love being part of a good cause, especially when they see their money goes 100 percent to educating students in a third-world country. I receive approximately twenty thousand dollars each year. Over the course of several years, that is sufficient to build two new schools in villages that have no school.

The Ugandan government will eventually approve the school once it is built, and the parents in the village have a short history of being organized and committed to their children's education. We have twenty-two such village schools under construction. Some are 90 percent completed, and for some, the foundation is being dug.

I get a response from my letter from about 65 percent of the recipients. I get anywhere from forty dollars to two thousand dollars in each letter. The fruit of this little project will go on for many, many generations. Those who give feel good that the fruits of their earnings, given to the poorest of the poor, produce great results. Those who receive, the children, receive a solid Catholic education from preschool through university, if they keep up their grades. Those who qualify for university are sponsored. Otherwise, they could never dream of even a high school education.

They are so appreciative of this gift. They never stop thanking, writing notes of appreciation, sending photos by email, and giving updates on their grades. My wish would be that all our donors could experience the overwhelming gratitude of our Uganda students.

What you are is God's gift to you. What you become is your gift to God.

—Anonymous

CHAPTER 22

FILLING THE GAP

Many Catholic families want the viable option of a Catholic education from preschool to college. When I arrived in Ocala in 1988, the parish had a good Catholic grade school and had begun a Catholic day care and preschool. But there was no mention of a Catholic high school. The nearest Catholic high school was close to one hundred miles away.

Due to our embarking on the Stewardship Way of Life, our Catholic grade school began to grow rapidly. Parents began anxiously pushing for a Catholic high school. To my mind, we were too small as a community, and we were surrounded by Catholic parishes with a high percentage of seniors. I could not foresee a Catholic high school, but God could.

I was led—by the Spirit, I believe—to contact the Lutheran pastor of St. John's Lutheran Church and School. Their high school was down to ninety-five students. By some chance, I asked if he might be interested in our sending our teens (ninth to twelfth grades) to his school. We wanted to teach the Catholic religion to our students while the rest of their student body took religion class from the Lutheran teachers. We would also want to say mass for our Catholic students once a month in one of their classrooms. He readily agreed.

As far as we knew, this agreement had never been attempted before or since. It all worked out exceedingly well. Our Catholic students were challenged and met the challenge very well. They grew in their Catholic faith. The student body at St. John's doubled and then almost tripled. This went on for seven years.

Our numbers were outgrowing St. John's. A survey strongly indicated Ocala and surrounding areas could now attempt to plan their own Catholic high school. There were many skeptics. The need was obvious; God had spoken. Because so many families were now convinced and were living by the Stewardship Way of Life, they readily went with God and supported the fund drive.

But before we ever engaged a professional fundraiser, we had quietly and privately raised or had pledges for $4 million. With the help of a fundraiser, we doubled that. We continued on our own from there and got up to $12 million. It was amazing. We still didn't have enough to move ahead, but the bishop, going against the advice of his own building and finance councils, gave the word to move ahead. God got to him too.

The school was built for a student body of six hundred with a completely outfitted football stadium, baseball stadium, and softball and soccer fields. As with the Catholic grade school, all Catholic families were free to enroll their students as long as they were fully stewardship families. That meant that from the beginning until now, twenty-two years later, none of them paid tuition. No one was ever denied a full Catholic education because of a lack of finances.

It has been proven over and over again that if we get the spirituality right, the money follows. It has been and it still is difficult for me to convince other pastors and diocesan officials that with the constant presentation of and renewal of the spirituality of the Stewardship Way of Life, money should never be a worry. It just works out. It takes an act of faith. It will not be worked out using math and surveys.

Trinity Catholic High School is a prime, concrete example that proves stewardship works. Presently, the school has no financial debt. Because we have added to the original school buildings four more classrooms, a field house, a new kitchen, and fourteen more acres of land, the total building cost of the school to date is in excess of $25 million. All that was paid off by March 2020.

If we could somehow quit our obsession with money and instead use our energy to convince people of the goodness and generosity of God, that He is the giver of all our blessings, then people would be much more available to God and return the first portion of His blessings. It is not a waste of time to pursue this course of action. It involves a lot of meaningful and fruitful work. And few, if any, have the guts to object, because it is 100 percent biblical.

All good giving and every perfect gift is from above.

—James 1:17

CHAPTER 23

UNEXPECTED HELP

During my first year as associate pastor at St. Joseph's in Lakeland, I noticed that the pastor, Father William O'Farrell, would periodically put a short notice in the church bulletin reminding people to put God somewhere in their last will and testament. He never spoke about it, just put it in the bulletin.

St. Joseph's seemed to get more wills and bequests than any parish I was familiar with, and it made sense. Our last will and testament is a major decision. Isn't God supposed to be in all our decisions? And why not in our last major decision? I picked up on this, especially over these last thirty-three years or so.

Most of our special projects (outside of our regular budget items) have been endowed in a huge way by major gifts left to the church in people's estates. While we have presented the whole idea of putting God, in some shape or fashion, into your will, we have never pushed or asked individuals to do it.

Here are a few examples of unusual gifts.

- A caretaker of a frail elderly man, Mr. Geary, living in a mobile home asked me to visit this man because, she said, his last will and testament made no sense. I did visit and told him it was none of my business where or to whom he was leaving his money. But since I had been called out to visit, I asked him if he minded telling me what he had decided.

He told me he was leaving his whole estate to a public school district in Massachusetts where he grew up so that the people would pay less taxes. I did not ask him the size of his estate, but I did tell him his old school district would not have their taxes reduced because of his gift. I suggested instead that he donated to his old parish in Massachusetts for the Catholic education of children whose parents could not afford tuition.

He said, "My old parish has no Catholic school."

"But," I said, "they must go to some Catholic schools in the area, so why don't I look up and call the pastor of the parish you grew up in and ask him if he has parishioners who want but could not afford a Catholic education?"

A few days later, I came back to Mr. Geary to let him know that the present pastor of the parish he grew up in would dearly love to be able to partially pay Catholic tuition for needy families. I gave Mr. Geary the formula for putting it in his will. He was happy about all that and said he would do it.

When I was departing, I said, "By the way, Mr. Geary, we have a Catholic school here at Blessed Trinity. Could you include our needy parents also?"

He said, "Yes, that's a great idea. I'll split it between both schools."

Years later, when he died, our Blessed Trinity school parents got $117,000, and Mr. Geary's old parish got $117,000. I put Mr. Geary's $117,000 into our school endowment fund. For over twenty-five years, we have been using only the interest earned on that gift to help families who cannot afford full Catholic tuition. The fruits of Mr. Geary's work on earth will go on for generations, because we don't have to touch the principal!

- Henrietta Pipkin, a devout French Canadian Catholic, was a very quiet, reserved woman of faith. I helped her once with a spiritual problem. I didn't do very much, but in her mind, she thought I saved her soul. Her relatives had drifted from her.

She did, at about age ninety, go to live with a relative up north. But in her letters, she hinted over and over that she was not happy up north. I was not reading between the lines.

Finally, I phoned her and asked, "Mrs. P, what do you want me to do? Do you want to come back to Florida?"

"Yes," she said. "I have been waiting for you to come and get me."

So I told her to pack her few things, and I would come on such a day, sneak her away to the airport, and fly with her down to South Florida to a retirement home she had requested to be in.

On the plane, the hostess asked what we wanted to drink—orange juice, water, tea, etc. Henrietta asked how much it cost. We told her it was free. She was so excited and told us she had not been given a glass of orange juice since she left Florida.

A finance planner met us in South Florida at her request. She signed over, in a charitable remainder trust, all her finances to Blessed Trinity, and she lived on the interest for the remainder of her life.

About a year or so later, in one of her letters, she asked why she was in South Florida and not in Ocala. I reminded her that she had requested that, but if she wanted to move to Ocala, I would come and get her. I did. We found a nice group of ladies to befriend her for her final few years in Ocala. She was truly happy and at peace.

Her estate, which gave the church over five hundred thousand dollars, was used entirely as a down payment for the construction of our day care and preschool, Angels in Arms. What a blessing Henrietta has been to thousands of little ones! Angels in Arms, over the last thirty-five years, has given a God-centered, loving foundation and a great start to between 200 and 250 children each year.

- A deaf man, Chester Dulecki, called me and tried to explain to me how he was a victim of elder abuse. He couldn't hear a word I said, so I told him I would visit him and his wife, Veronica, in their retirement home. In addition to being deaf, Chester had very poor eyesight. Veronica was unable to talk. Someone with knowledge of their disabilities had reported that Chester was abusing his wife.

  I asked Veronica a series of questions, which Chester couldn't hear anyway, and Veronica answered by using her right hand for yes and her left hand for no. I was thoroughly convinced, beyond a shadow of a doubt, that Chester and Veronica truly loved each other. There was not a hint of any abuse. So I told them I would get them an attorney. They would need legal help to prove that Chester was not incompetent and was quite capable of caring for himself, Veronica, and their finances.

  Unknown to me, someone was suspicious of my visit to Chester and listened outside the door. Since I had to use a high-pitched voice to get through to Chester, this concerned person heard every word and reported me to the bishop. I convinced the bishop that Chester needed assistance, and we, as a church, had a duty to help with the use of an attorney.

  With the attorney's help, Chester's ears were cleaned out, and he was prepared for his day in court. Veronica was now in the hospital. The judge concluded that Chester was of sound mind, maybe even more balanced than the judge himself! Chester was declared fully in charge of Veronica and of all his affairs. Veronica died the next day.

  Money was never discussed between Chester and the church; however, he immediately transferred $100,000 to our high school. Then he put $250,000 in trust for the school. He came to mass every day with the help of one of the parishioners.

> He longed to leave this earth and be at home with the Lord and Veronica. He used to ask why the Lord wasn't taking him. So he decided he would transfer the rest of his estate to the church, and maybe that would speed up the Lord's call.
>
> Their names are now on the field house at TCHS. Overall, he and Veronica left over five hundred thousand to Catholic education.

It is all further evidence for me that if we let God be God and continue to let God lead us, we need never worry about the results. We have to be alert. It can be very easy to let a God thing pass by. God, all too often, speaks softly. We have to be ready to seize the moment and open the door, and God does the rest.

For I was hungry and you gave me food. I was thirsty and you gave me drink, a stranger and you welcomed me, naked and clothed me, ill and you cared for me, in prison and you visited me.

—Matthew 6:35–36

CHAPTER 24

GOD'S LOUDEST VOICE

How could we ever escape God's clearest and loudest voice call us to take care of Him in and through our outreach to the poor? It is all over Scripture, God's holy Word. We have the story of the Good Samaritan (Luke 10:23–37), of Zacchaeus ("Half of my possessions I give to the poor" [Luke 1:10]), of the rich young man and Lazarus (Luke 19:19–31), of riches in heaven (Luke 12:32–34), of the rich fool (Luke 12:13–21), and of the final judgment (Matthew 25:31–46). Both the Old and New Testaments call us to be our brothers' keeper. It begins with the story of Cain and Abel in Genesis and goes right through to Judgment Day. Nowhere in the Bible does it ever say that anyone for any reason should be excluded from our care and outreach.

God's voice comes through and is heard by many thousands of people and businesses as they reach out to provide an uplift to the have-nots of this world. This is done privately, outside organized efforts, by people who come across a needy person. It is done mostly through organizations like the Society of Saint Vincent de Paul, Food for the Poor, Brother's Keeper at Blessed Trinity, Saving Mercy for the homeless in Ocala, Catholic Relief Services Worldwide, etc. What amazes me the most is, while God's voice in this matter is loud and clear, we still have all too many who ignore His voice and even some who have the courage to object to our helping anyone outside our country.

All my life as a priest, I have never been in a parish that doesn't have a strong ministry or outreach to the have-nots. Help for the poor cannot be in the budget a year in advance. That's what happens in some religions. The poor are turned away because it is not in the budget or the budget has been spent already. There is always room and resources to respond to all legitimate requests for the poor.

We do not have to go through a committee to help the poor. I always have money to respond, a special fund. And no matter how many come for help to draw from that fund, others send in money for a needy cause. That special fund for the poor never dries up.

More than once, I have been in my office with an appointment. Then the phone rings, and the person is asking for $1,500 to catch up on rent or be kicked out. My appointment overhears the conversation and immediately says, "I'll cover that." Or I get a special donation in the mail from someone as a Thanksgiving offering to God for blessings received, and close to the same day, sometimes the same hour, I get a request for the very same amount from a desperate person in financial need.

Hearing God's voice appealing to us through the poor should be an easy challenge for us. Also, when we do respond, we should feel happy that we have listened to God's voice and served Him in and through the poor.

Section V

Go into the World

We must be careful not to limit God's wisdom, for it is infinite, we must not limit His power for it is omnipotent, we must not limit His mercy, for it is as high as heaven. But He will perform His word, honor our faith and reward them that diligently seek Him.

—Charles Haddon Spurgeon

Chapter 25

God Is Able

Three IHMR Sisters from Uganda came to our parish, Blessed Trinity, Ocala, in 2000. We were and are truly blessed to have them ministering in a great variety of ways over the years. They have taught in our school, worked in the health clinic, and assisted in our outreach to the poor, among other duties.

Sister Juliet, while teaching religion students at Blessed Trinity Elementary School, showed a fellow teacher a photo of a stick/mud Catholic church in her home village of Nalweyo, Uganda. This teacher shared it with her third-grade students, who thought the building was not good enough, so they started selling T-shirts to raise money for a real church for Sister Juliet's home community. The project gained steam throughout the school community.

The parish then got involved. The bishop of the Diocese of Hoima—Nalweyo was part of his diocese—heard about the effort. He had a vision of making Nalweyo the center of a future parish, so he requested that the future, permanent new church be increased from the original three-hundred-seat capacity to five-hundred-seat capacity, and before final plans were drawn up, he increased the capacity to eight hundred.

Blessed Trinity, Ocala, rose to the occasion and in no time (about a year) raised $85,000, which was the original budget to complete the church. We requested that the new church be named Blessed Trinity, and we officially adopted it as our sister parish. We had no plans to do anything more than building a permanent church for Sister Juliet's home community, but God had big plans, big plans that were only revealed to us little by little over the years and are still being revealed to us.

Seventeen of us planned a visit to the new Blessed Trinity Church in Nalweyo for the grand opening and blessing by Bishop Deogratias. We were primarily tourists. We were met at Entebbe Airport by Bishop Deogratias and other leaders. The hospitality we received over the next ten days was just way, way above and beyond any expectations we had in advance. We were treated to trips to the shrine of the Uganda martyrs, Murchison Falls National Park, a boat ride on the river Nile, and a visit to the US Embassy and to the residence of Cardinal Emmanuel and the local king.

When we finally got to the new Blessed Trinity Church, we found it to be much bigger and more impressive than we had expected. But while it had walls and a roof, it had no permanent floor or windows or doors or pews. It took another $65,000 of fundraising to complete the church.

The mass consecrating the church was very sacred, uplifting, and memorable! There were baptisms, weddings, lots of speeches during mass, and two great processions—one with the book of the Gospels and one bringing up the gifts at the offertory. The mass took more than four hours and was followed by local and professional entertainers, and the celebrations concluded with a soccer game.

We left Uganda filled with joy, excitement, and enthusiasm to go back to Ocala and raise the remaining $65,000 to finish the construction of the church. Once we completed that, we had no further plans for our sister parish, except to keep up a good, ongoing relationship with them.

On the way to and from Entebbe Airport and all during our tours, I noticed dozens and dozens and dozens of taxi vans, many of them crowned with a big, easy-to-read sign front and back: God Is Able. That sign hit my brain and left an indelible mark. It said a lot to me about what God was doing or trying to do in my life. It is the only suggestion that haunts me as a suitable title for this book.

We cannot all do great things. But we can do small things with great love.

—St. Teresa of Calcutta

CHAPTER 26

UGANDA REVISITED

In 2007, I revisited Blessed Trinity, Nalweyo, Uganda, primarily to see the completion of their new church and to visit their new pastor, Father Joachim. Blessed Trinity, Nalweyo, was made a new parish, split off from the mother parish, Our Lady of the Rosary, Kakindo. It was also given seventeen villages, which they called subparishes.

This time, I was no longer a tourist. Father Joachim got me fully involved in daily masses and celebration of many baptisms, and there also, I celebrated my first Ugandan wedding. Little did I know then that in future visits, I would baptize thousands of children and officiate at dozens of marriages.

During the second visit, our Ocala Blessed Trinity parish promised to raise funds to build a priests' house (presbytery), rebuild two classrooms to begin their Blessed Trinity Primary School, and help them build and open a medical clinic in the mother parish, Our Lady of the Rosary, Kakindo. With those promises in place, I almost got away. But they wouldn't let me go until I visited one of their subparishes, St. Peter's, Katikati, on the way to the airport. Actually, it was only about four kilometers away.

There I saw—and I'll never forget it—on a rainy day eighty-five students at school under the trees with four uncertified teachers. They had one little mud-and-straw hut for a building. They begged for a real building where they could celebrate mass on Sundays when a priest was available (then just once a month) and use it as a school during the week.

I believed we already had taken on too much, but God knew better. Back in Ocala, I asked Mrs. Jean Corr if she would give $25,000 for the building. She did, and during my next visit to Nalweyo, we blessed the building Mrs. Corr had paid for. We had over twenty baptisms and over two thousand people present. Since then, Mrs. Corr has built them a seven-hundred-seat church, given them a deep freshwater well, and continued the building out of the school, which now has over four hundred students with some boarders. And that is just one subparish.

The new parish has grown from seventeen to thirty-two subparishes. We have been able to find sponsors or funds to complete thirty permanent new churches. The thirty-first one is under construction, and they are trying to secure the land and begin construction for the thirty-second one. We have built or have under construction twenty-two elementary schools and have completed one 650-student secondary school. We have built six dorms with 150 students (approximately) in each dorm for boys and girls from P3 up to S6.

We have drilled forty 180-foot-deep freshwater wells, at least one in each subparish. The priests' house has been expanded to house four priests and space for guests. We have built a staff house with twenty-one bedrooms for teachers and visitors. We have repaired and built a new building at a local orphanage.

The new medical clinic in Kakindo has a staff of twelve, and it includes a maternity ward with capacity for up to twelve new mothers, along with an operating room for minor surgeries and offices to receive and give medical assistance to outpatients. We also bought the parish a 120-acre farm. St. James's Farm dedicates twenty acres to crops and the rest for livestock with a farm manager.

We published a 120-page pictorial directory on our sister parish during the COVID-19 shutdown in 2020. That directory has greatly expanded the interest in and the increase of new sponsors to our sister parish. People easily see that this is God in action. They see results. They know that 100 percent of their donations go directly to improving the quality of the spiritual, educational, and health of people. Nothing is spent on flights, on staff, on office expenses, etc.

People feel good that they are making a positive contribution to the quality of life of at least some people. They can readily see it fulfills God's holy Word and the challenge He gave us when He said in Proverbs 3:9, "Honor the Lord with your wealth, with first fruits of all you produce, then will your barn be filled with plenty, with new wine your vats will overflow."

For it is in giving
that we receive.

—Prayer of
St. Francis of Assisi

CHAPTER 27

WHAT RETURN CAN I MAKE?

While our Ocala parish has improved the lives of thousands of people in our sister parish, Nalweyo, Uganda, it certainly is not a one-way street. Over three hundred people have gone to Uganda since our initial visit in 2004. Most annual group visits have approximately twenty missionaries. They range in age from sixteen to eighty-three.

They include high school students, college students, pharmacists, teachers, carpenters, nuns, coaches, computer experts, RNs, doctors, dentists, priests, painters, farmers, counselors, and retired people. Many go back again and again. Over 99 percent come back with a new enthusiasm for living the life God has called them into and for passing on that positive energy to others.

Thousands more at home are growing spiritually not only by sharing their finances but also by collecting much-needed items for the sister parish, such as schoolbooks, pencils, paper, laptops, farm tools, soccer balls, T-shirts, kids' clothes, toothbrushes, and shoes, especially soccer shoes. We have succeeded in shipping two forty-foot containers filled with two tractors, an automobile, a disc harrow, plough, wheelchairs, walkers, farm tools, carpenter tools, thousands of pairs of shoes, clothes, soccer uniforms, etc.

Each missionary who goes is allowed one checked bag with their own personal items and two checked bags filled with items for the mission, one of which has to be paid for. In all our annual visits to Uganda, we have never been asked at the airport to pay any duty on the items we bring in. Just about anyone and everyone can make a positive contribution to the mission.

Three people have already left a large portion of their estate to our Nalweyo mission. Combined, this amounts to over $750,000. All this has happened and continues to happen, and no one but God has a clear idea of where it is all leading to or if there is some kind of a conclusion down the road to all this involvement between Blessed Trinity, Ocala, and Blessed Trinity, Nalweyo, Uganda.

One thing is clear, however: when you allow God to do His thing, no one but Him knows the final outcome.

Commit your way to the
Lord; trust that God will act.

—Psalm 37:5

CHAPTER 28

CAPE TOWN BLESSINGS

Ricarda "Ricci" Gaudin, a foreign exchange student from Germany, graduated from Trinity Catholic High School in Ocala in 2006. Her brother Gregor also graduated in 2007. I helped Ricci some but not a whole lot during her year, but to her, it was a big help. I got to know her family a little during graduation ceremonies.

Ricci kept in touch with me by letters and cards over the next ten years. Even once, while I had a four-hour layover in Munich, she picked me up at the airport and showed me downtown Munich, and we had a German lunch. Ricci and her family are Lutherans.

Three or four years ago, my last letter to Ricci was returned. She had moved, but she still had my phone number, which never changed. She phoned me in the fall of 2021 and told me she was engaged, and in her dream wedding, she had me as the priest.

I said to her, "Ricci, you are Lutheran, and besides, I could not sign a legal marriage license in Germany."

Ricci replied, "Here in Germany, we get married by the state first. And since I am already legally married, you have no problem. Also, my religious ceremony is not in Germany. Eighty of my family and the groom's family and our friends have paid for a beautiful wedding destination in Cape Town, South Africa. And you do not need anyone's permission, because it is not a Catholic wedding, and it is not in a church!"

My wheels started turning. Because of COVID-19, I had not been to our sister parish in Uganda for two years. Schools in Uganda were about to reopen after being closed for two years. Would it be possible for me to go to Cape Town for two days and then to the mission in Uganda for a week?

"Ricci, I'll phone you back once I find out if flights can be arranged."

Somehow, all the flights could be arranged to suit the time I had available.

Forty-three years earlier, I had met another German exchange student, Andreas Groos, in Lakeland, where he was a student at Florida Southern College. He had a very strong Catholic faith. He became very active in our Catholic Newman Club. I got him to be a minister of the Eucharist while he was in Lakeland.

He and I have been in regular communication over the last forty-three years. He is married with three grown daughters and one son. His daughter Antonia came to our parish in Ocala for six months in the fall of 2013 when she was a college student. Andreas became a doctor, a well-known urologist, but stayed very down-to-earth, humble, and a devout Catholic.

He responded to my Christmas greetings in 2021 with a nice letter in mid-January 2022. I replied with another letter telling of my newer German connection, a bride who also was now a medical doctor, and that I had planned to officiate at her religious wedding in Cape Town on February 7. February 7 was only two weeks away.

Andreas got my letter two days before my departure. He tracked me down by phone, all excited, letting me know he and his wife were flying into Cape Town for a vacation the day before me, and surely, we could meet for a meal.

I was free to meet Andreas and Anne, his wife, on Sunday morning, February 8, but I worried about mass. What to do? The wedding party was either all Lutherans or no religion. So I asked Andreas if we could participate in mass somewhere before our meal. He was delighted.

The RC church was a four-minute walk from this Cape Town home that he had purchased recently. The priest at mass was a Dutch man. He invited me to concelebrate. During mass, I couldn't stop reflecting on how it was possible for me to be concelebrating mass all the way down in Cape Town with friends of mine from Hamburg, Germany, whom I had not met in person for many years! Yes, God, thank You again. With You, all things are possible.

Dr. Andreas told me he was going to write a book entitled *Catholic Mass 52 Sundays of the Year*. It would contain a personal story from fifty-two different families. And now he had one more Sunday covered since he was putting our meeting for mass in St. Margaret Mary Church, Cape Town, for the fifth Sunday in ordinary time 2022.

Dr. Andreas also told me that a highlight of his Catholic life was that he had been a minister of the Eucharist for forty-three years. He was thrilled by the fact that he had greeted people at Communion time with the body of Christ more often than all the "Hello!" and "How are you?" and "Nice to meet you!" greetings put together over the last forty-three years.

I do not worry in advance about what I am going to include in my homily at weddings since I have officiated at over three thousand of them, but this wedding was different. There were no Catholics that I was aware of. Thank God the bride had chosen 1 Corinthians, St. Paul's great passage on love.

I let God do His thing. We had some interaction with the guests and wedding party during the homily. They seemed to wake up based on the topic that God was love and that we were to spend our lives returning His love. How could they not join in? And marriage was to be the most intimate way of imitating God's love.

Many told me afterward that we hit the nail on the head. Back home in Germany, they didn't go to church. Or if they did, they just politely attended while the priest did his thing. Two dating couples in particular told me they now had a different focus for planning their future together in marriage and not just living together with no thought of marriage.

One beautiful custom I witnessed the bride and groom carry out—others do it too—was that as they drove by all the rich tourist spots in Cape Town, they would come across beggars along the way, and they would let down one window and hand out an already-made food package that was left over from one of their meals. No food was wasted.

I said to myself, "Could we do that in Ocala?"

Cape Town was beautiful—mighty, picturesque mountains surrounding a very long, very fertile wine valley. The bride put me up on a farm, which was really a very attractive group of cottages with all the hotel luxuries. I had to travel by taxi to and from the wedding venue each day. It was twenty minutes away. Three of the four taxi drivers were more than anxious to talk religion.

One man from Zimbabwe was married (civilly) to a Catholic wife, and why not in the Catholic church? He had just completed putting his dowry together. I was familiar with that necessity in our mission in Uganda. He was now ready for a Catholic wedding, but he was not part of any particular religion.

I gave him a nice wedding gift (in dollars) and gave him a message for his Catholic wife. She was to stay strong in the practice of her Catholic faith and let God do His thing, and rest assured, her husband would join her in the faith in the future!

The husband laughed and said, "You are probably right."

I didn't know what to expect in advance for my two and a half days in Cape Town. Maybe that was a blessing. It was best to just be available, try not to miss any God-given opportunities, and then let God be God. Thank you, God.

CONCLUSION

God spoke, somehow, to all the prophets of the Old Testament. They recorded their encounters with God. A prophet isn't just one who deals with the future. He, especially, is a teacher, a voice, or a spokesperson for and from God. Through him, God speaks, mostly about the present. He refers to the past so we can learn from it and, from there, be more ready to listen to God directing us and encouraging us to be more focused on Him in the present.

All of us are meant to be prophets/teachers one way or another. We may never have a pulpit or a classroom or children, but nevertheless, we are meant to be the voice of God to some people along the way.

While I was called by God to be His voice, whether from the pulpit or in the classroom or at board meetings or in marriage preparation for couples or in the annual Catholic inquiry class or in the confessional, yet God spoke to me through various people he sent to me along the way. Many of them are still living, so I won't name them.

One person in particular, now passed on from this life, was God's voice to me for thirty years. Ms. Fran Harwas, on a weekly basis, sounded out for me the voice or the call of God in many of the day-to-day, ordinary events and maybe the not so ordinary.

Frequently, she would remark, "That's a *God thing*! It is not just a coincidence! Count yourself blessed!"

And as other events cropped up, she would say, "There He (God) goes again!"

What do I hope and pray you will bring away from reading this book? Hopefully, it will inspire you to be very convinced that God is very present and very active in your own life. Hopefully, you will see that some people are sent by God into your life to get your attention. That could be your spouse or your child or a friend or an inspired speaker. Hopefully, also, you will be convinced that God is very much calling you to be His mouthpiece, His voice, not just within your family but also in your place of work or on the playing field or at a party.

If reading this book has caused you to reflect on where God has gotten through to you in your life or where God has tried and you have not been available to listen, then I am happy that my little effort has not been in vain. I know writing the various chapters of this book has sharpened my own focus and has caused me to pray about being more present and more open to God.

May the voice of the good Lord, through you, uplift your sphere of influence in the place where you are presently planted.

About the Author

Father Patrick J. Sheedy, known as Father Pat, is the fourth of twelve children born in Cooraclare County, Clare, Ireland. He was ordained with his brother, Father Michael (RIP), in his local village church on June 13, 1965.

Father Pat never intended to author a book. His only ambition was—and still is—to be a parish priest trying, by God's grace, to respond to people's spiritual needs on all levels. During the shutdown for COVID-19, reflecting on the years of his priesthood, he saw clearly that if God made His plan clearly known and a person threw his faith and talents into God's plan, mighty results followed every time.

In brief, when God is allowed to be God, there is always a whole lot to write about that would grab the attention of anyone seeking God.

Despite being an introvert by nature, most are convinced Father Pat is an extrovert. For the most part, he has been unable to say no when God made Himself clear. This has brought Father Pat to a great variety of projects, missions, and movements that he had never foreseen or planned or dreamed of.

After fifty-eight years of priesthood, Father Pat, still in great health, enjoys a ten-hour workday. His major hobby is enjoying seeing God in action every day, even on his days off on Mondays.

www.ingramcontent.com/pod-product-compliance
Lightning Source LLC
Chambersburg PA
CBHW031321160726
47993CB00001B/497
9798889605812